Imagine the possibilities when international education becomes truly inclusive. The ability to make connections with people from every corner of the world, embracing new cultures, perspectives, and ideas, is now a fundamental part of life. The authors of Becoming a Totally Inclusive School have turned their personal experiences and views into a source of inspiration for people who strive to make international education more accessible and more effective for all.

Jane Larsson, Executive Director,
Council of International Schools (CIS)

Real-life, accessible, challengingly upfront and honest, Becoming a Totally Inclusive School is essential reading for all educators. In these times where awareness of diversity, equity and inclusion are front and centre for us all, we need resources that support us in facing sometimes uncomfortable truths; where we look at ourselves and our communities and ask, "Is everyone totally included in our school, is our school totally inclusive?" Angeline, Sadie and Stephen have created a book that covers key theoretical models and approaches, alongside practical case studies in action that can be used and implemented in schools throughout the world.

Liz Free, Director, International School Rheintal, Switzerland

A clear and accessible framework for reflection and action for social justice. Becoming a Totally Inclusive School is a must-read for any educator or school leader who is ready and willing to lean into the deep work of cultivating a learning community that is diverse, equitable, and inclusive.

Elizabeth Palathra, Primary Teacher, Switzerland

Becoming a Totally Inclusive School

Educators are at a crossroads and the global call for institutions to address their inequitable structures is ringing loudly. For teachers and school leaders who are hearing that call, this book offers knowledge and guidance for becoming a Totally Inclusive school.

Each chapter delves into key ideas that are fundamental to addressing the complex challenge of achieving Total Inclusivity — one which encompasses and values racial diversity, gender equality, LGBTQ+ inclusivity, neurodiversity and more. Across the three sections, the authors introduce key terms and concepts important to inclusivity, focused on mindsets, behaviours and systems and structures. Explore how interactions contribute to or impede progress, and engage with tools, stories and reflection points to translate knowledge into practice.

Written in an accessible style with reflective exercises in every chapter, the book will guide educational professionals along the pathway to becoming advocates for inclusivity in their schools and communities.

Angeline Aow is an international school educator, teacher trainer and pedagogical leader. She trained and taught as a teacher in Sydney, Australia, and began her international school career in China. She has worked at the Berlin International School, Germany, since 2005 and is an international advisor with the Council of International Schools, developing and facilitating services in support of inclusion via diversity, equity and anti-racism. www.angelineaow.com

Sadie Hollins has worked previously as the head of sixth form at a British International School based in Thailand. She is the creator and editor of the *Wellbeing in International Schools Magazine* and has written for a number of different educational blogs.

Stephen Whitehead is a British sociologist and educationalist. He is an internationally recognised expert on men and masculinities, gender identity and international education. This is his 16th book, and his third on Total Inclusivity. Stephen lives with his wife in Chiang Mai, Thailand. www.stephen-whitehead.com

ANGELINE AOW, SADIE HOLLINS
AND STEPHEN WHITEHEAD

Becoming a Totally Inclusive School

A Guide for Teachers and School Leaders

Routledge
Taylor & Francis Group

LONDON AND NEW YORK

Cover image: © Xoài David

First published 2023
by Routledge
4 Park Square, Milton Park, Abingdon, Oxon OX14 4RN

and by Routledge
605 Third Avenue, New York, NY 10158

Routledge is an imprint of the Taylor & Francis Group, an informa business

British Library Cataloguing-in-Publication Data
A catalogue record for this book is available from the British Library

ISBN: 978-1-032-13677-6 (hbk)
ISBN: 978-1-032-13674-5 (pbk)
ISBN: 978-1-003-23123-3 (ebk)

DOI: 10.4324/9781003231233

Typeset in Joanna MT
by SPi Technologies India Pvt Ltd (Straive)

Contents

FIGURES

TABLES

Acknowledgements

Angeline: This book is for each student who has the right to walk into a school building without leaving their identity at the school gate. What we owe our students is within our grasp and only possible with educators committed to creating Totally Inclusive schools. I am thankful for educators dedicated to serving students under their care and acknowledge that we are all on a journey to know better and do better.

I am grateful for these educators for the feedback they provided on aspects of the book and for supporting thinking throughout my writing process: Alysa Perreras, Dr. Danau Tanu, Elizabeth Palathra, Harriett Dukes, Jane Larsson, Jennifer Abrams, Jessica Wei Huang, Joel Jr Llaban, Katierose Deos, Liz Free, Dr. Megel Barker, Nunana Nyomi and Tricia Friedman.

Thank you, Xoài David, for collaborating with me to create meaningful cover art that brought to life a powerful metaphor for what we are aspiring to achieve.

I am grateful that through Stephen, I was introduced to Sadie. Without you, Sadie, this book would not be possible. Thank you for our Sunday morning conversations. Without you and Laura, this book would not have been birthed.

Writing this book while leading and teaching during a pandemic would not have been possible without the support of my husband who has kept our household and lives running. Vielen Dank mein Lieber. All three of my boys teach me every day how to be a better human being. Our eldest; your intellectual disability teaches me every day what it means to be inclusive. Our youngest, may you grow to be a feminist, anti-racist, anti-ableist, LGBTQ+ ally and continue to be the principled, kind, caring activist you already are.

Sadie: I am forever grateful to my wife, Laura, who has supported, encouraged and believed in me. This book wouldn't have been possible without you. The process of writing this book has helped me to grow more than I could have ever imagined, and I am most grateful to Angeline for the vision and creativity she has brought to this process – I have learnt so much from you. Finally, I am thankful to all the educators and leaders who were on this journey before us and to those who are here with us now.

Stephen: First, I would like to acknowledge the Routledge team who helped turn the Total Inclusivity concept into books: Katie Peace, Kendrick Loo and Yong Ling Lam. Second, my thanks to all the many individuals who have been part of my journey as an educationalist (lecturer, researcher, writer) into issues pertaining to diversity, equity, inclusion and justice in and outside of education and over many years. And finally, to my students; thanks for what you taught me.

Total Inclusivity and You
Section I

Chapter One

Why are you an educator? What does this professional identity mean to you? These are questions you have probably asked yourself at some point. Almost certainly you'll have been reflecting recently on why you continue with one of the most demanding of jobs – made all the more stressful by a global pandemic.

We don't know why you are an educator or what that means to you, indeed we don't even know if you are an educator. But one thing we do know – you care enough about people to want to bring about diversity, equity, inclusion and justice for all.

How do we know this? Because that can be the only possible reason to pick up this book and start reading it.

You want Total Inclusivity even if right now you're not sure what it is, what it entails, and what it will demand of you, both personally and professionally. You feel a sense of urgency to advocate for and take action towards Total Inclusivity.

Before we get into that, perhaps it's helpful to share a little bit about us, the authors, and why this work is so important to us.

Angeline, Sadie and Stephen crossed paths in late 2020, and after a series of serendipitous events (and the magic of social media), we came together with the goal and purpose of writing a book that would represent our shared passions of promoting inclusivity in education. This is the result.

So who are we?

Angeline is an Australian Chinese migrant and international educator who was born in Malaysia to parents who came from very different backgrounds. Her father's family had fled from political turmoil in China to Malaysia to find themselves a new home, and her mother has Hakka roots. Her family background and experience have caused her to reflect on the complex issues of social class, the cultural expectations placed on women who married into wealthier families and the

DOI: 10.4324/9781003231233-2

caregiving responsibilities upheld in traditional Chinese family structures. Angeline's journey has brought her into the world of international education, and her experiences as a multi-ethnic migrant have shaped her work on promoting women's leadership in education, identity, intersectionality and inclusivity (Aow, 2021).

Sadie is a British-born LGBTQ+ international educator who previously worked in higher education in the UK, and has held a leadership role at an international school in Thailand. Prior to her work in international education, she spent a brief but transformative time working in the world of international addiction treatment, based at the world's first LGBTQ+-specific addiction treatment programme outside of the US. For her, this is where the importance of the different aspects of identity in health and recovery first became overwhelmingly clear. Inspired by this time working in the addiction field, Sadie has become passionate about exploring issues relating to wellbeing within the international school context, in which identity takes a central place.

Stephen is a British-born gender and sexuality researcher, with a career-long passion for exploring the depths of men and masculinities. Stephen has written extensively about the intersecting nature of gender, sexuality, management and education. His research and writing have sought to explain how we can resolve one of the biggest challenges facing humankind; the erasure of traditional masculine values and behaviours, otherwise known as hegemonic (toxic) masculinity. Never has there been a more important time to bring insight into those ways of being a man which are problematic, if not deadly, for all of us, including the men who behave like this.

We each bring a different life experience and understanding to the idea of Total Inclusivity. Our collective drive towards making education not just representative of a diverse workplace but also reflective of the diversity throughout the world is made explicit in the book's key aims:

1. To bring together the existing work being done in all areas of inclusivity in education; anti-racism, LGBTQ+ inclusion, cultural awareness, and gender equity
2. To provide an accessible and informative text that identifies some of the key issues relating to Total Inclusivity and provides advice on how to address covert and overt discrimination in schools

3. To offer a practical guide towards Total Inclusivity that remains relevant across domestic and international educational curriculums and systems

The book aims to engage all members of the educational community, including those whose identity construct means that they may not have experienced discrimination first-hand. We all know that it's easier to advocate for change when something directly affects us, but we also know that for change to be meaningful and long lasting, it needs to involve everyone.

And we acknowledge those readers who, by virtue of their intersectional identity, are already well versed in the issues we explore and detail in this book; racism, homophobia, implicit bias, microaggressions, sexual identities, violence, and white privilege in schools, education, and elsewhere.

This book is designed to provide you with both a theoretical and practical basis for being the best, most inclusive, educator that you can be. Because there can be little doubt, as the 21st century unfolds, that we are going to need you. The students in your classes right now, whether online or in person, need you. What happens, or does not happen, in our classrooms not only greatly influences a student's future but also the future of education as a whole.

This is why we, Angeline, Sadie and Stephen, bring ourselves to this book as people and professionals with disparate backgrounds but with the same common goal:

> The creation of a global educational system that is truly, and in every respect, equitable, diverse, inclusive and enabling of social justice

THE DEFINITION

To turn Total Inclusivity into a social justice action that leaders, teachers, students and parents can participate in, we need a simple but powerful definition. And this is it:

> Total Inclusivity means recognising, valuing, protecting and nurturing diverse identities, including those of race, gender, sexual orientation, class, disability, age, religion and language.

If you recognise the inherent worthiness of that intention, if it speaks to both your heart and your head, then you are on your way to being an advocate for Total Inclusivity and have taken a step towards becoming a Totally Inclusive School.

THE MOMENTUM

The last few decades have witnessed momentum building towards something incredibly important; a recognition that the world can and should be better than it is. A desire for Total Inclusivity. Increasingly, seemingly isolated incidents of discrimination and violence have led to global protests and overwhelming calls for structural and individual change. The #MeToo movement that gained worldwide exposure following the shocking revelations surrounding Harvey Weinstein in 2017. The growing global momentum of the Black Lives Matter movement, particularly following the murders of George Floyd and Breonna Taylor. The "Trans Rights Are Human Rights" campaign in 2020. These events, to name a few, have brought issues of diversity, equity, inclusion and justice (DEIJ) to the forefront of public awareness. However, it is also important to acknowledge that these movements have very long histories which precede the current momentum, and there have been many movements and leaders and much research which have informed this current work and from which this book draws.

History is synonymous with discrimination, for there is no escaping the fact that different historically marginalised groups and identities have traditionally received exclusionary treatment and continue to face unspeakable oppression. Change must happen, and that starts with every single one of us. It's time to get comfortable with being uncomfortable – because that is where change comes.

Now, more than ever, it feels like our collective consciousness and attention are focused on the need for change – not just change in our personal beliefs and actions but also at the structural level. And where better to start than in schools? Schools are where we learn how to read and write, where we learn how to make and repair friendships and where we grow to become citizens in and of the world. In addition to family and home, schools are important places where identities get formed. Schools are where we start the journey of becoming who we want to be. Schools are also microcosms of wider society. Nothing exists in a vacuum – not our behaviour, not the behaviour of our colleagues and students and not the behaviour of our leadership or organisation.

People want change and schools need to be that change.

There has been an explosion of individuals and organisations on social media platforms (and off social media), committed to fighting for DEIJ at local, national and international levels, committed to ensuring these principles are incorporated (and implemented) into organisational policies and practices, committed to dismantling and decolonising curriculums and committed to educating students through whole-school approaches to inclusion.

Around the world, an increasing number of schools are now grappling with the complexities and challenges of implementing anti-racist, pro-LGBTQ+, gender-equitable, non-discriminatory curriculums, policies and practices. This book is for all these schools and will guide you, the reader, towards the creation of a Totally Inclusive School.

So what does Total Inclusivity really look like in a school setting? Why do schools, staff and students need it? After all, there is a lot of good work already being done by many different groups and educators to improve DEIJ in schools, promote the visibility of women in education, to promote anti-racism and work towards better LGBTQ+ inclusion and discussion in schools. Why the need for 'Total Inclusivity', and how can it be embedded into the fabric of a school?

The aim of *Becoming a Totally Inclusive School* is to provide both knowledge and practical guidance for implementing this concept into the daily life of any school, anywhere. The hope is that you, the reader, will follow the Total Inclusivity values, principles and advice laid out in the chapters ahead and become not only fully familiar with the concept but also confident in putting this into practice in your own professional setting. Whatever your relationship to education, be you a teacher, school leader or administrator, you should be able to recognise and personally embrace the values of Total Inclusivity both personally and professionally. This then leads us to the most important objective which is for each member of every school community to become an advocate for Total Inclusivity.

THE COMMUNITY

As the adage goes, 'it takes a village to raise a child'. For many students, schools provide that village, that community. They assume the responsibility of raising that child to become a happy, resilient and fulfilled member of society. And now, more than ever, that community needs to be Totally Inclusive. You need only look into the not-so-distant past to see the integral place that schools hold in many students' lives. During the period of global lockdown due to the COVID-19 pandemic, there was relentless critical commentary across social media: 'Teachers are lazy'…. 'Teachers just got 6 months off work'…. 'Teachers want schools to stay shut … they don't care about the kids.'

Anyone who works within education knows how misdirected these statements were.

The reality is, despite fearing for their own wellbeing, as well as the wellbeing of their families, teachers worked tirelessly on the front line throughout the pandemic. In order to provide schooling to the most vulnerable students or the children of frontline workers, they went to work as planned, sanitising desks and equipment, delivering lessons simultaneously online and in person and even supervising the COVID testing of students. More than ever, schools proved that they are often the primary community that a child is a part of. Schools became the community that students needed when the world was in crisis. They provided not only education but also vital childcare, healthcare and mental health support. If the pandemic has taught us anything it's taught us the value of teachers. Without teachers, there is no school.

Never has there been a better opportunity to evaluate the school communities that we are a part of and ask ourselves, once the pandemic dust starts to settle, if we are creating and growing a school into a community that is Totally Inclusive.

Community is a compelling term, and arguably one of the most important words in the English language.

The *Cambridge Dictionary* (online) defines *community* as:

all the people who live in a particular area, or a group of people who are considered as a unit because of their shared interests or background.

Clearly, the concept of 'community' is highly subjective and complex. However, the principles of commonality, association and shared identity are central, and that is what we are calling for schools to provide — spaces that enable students, staff and families to create and foster positive emotional connections to others. Yet, in modern-day society, these connections have become increasingly worn and frayed, not least because we have allowed ourselves to prioritise other issues.

Let's consider, for example, our obsession with 'results'. Any teacher reading this knows that many schools have become fixated on results, what we describe elsewhere as 'performativity' in education: targets, league tables, measurables, performance indicators (Whitehead, 2022; Ball, 2003; Dent & Whitehead, 2001).

As the pressure to ensure academic success has increased, schools have had to make difficult decisions about what to prioritise, and as such, many forms of prejudice and discrimination have been left unchecked. If you doubt that, just look at the number of highly prestigious schools around the world, delivering perfect exam results, standing accused of racism, sexual abuse and a host of other violences against their students and staff.

When school leaders fail to see the realities of their school culture and prioritise exam results as the most worthwhile 'measurable', then something is seriously amiss.

Professional and personal relationships have never been more important than they are today, not least because we are currently in the middle of a global wellbeing crisis, one that is having a dramatic and adverse impact on students and teachers. If that were not enough, we are seeing increasing evidence of discourses of misogyny, racism, antisemitism, antifeminism, homophobia, sexual violence and conspiracy theories spreading online via far-right platforms (Hall, 2021).

Despite all this, we're not asking any less of our students, or teachers, in terms of the demands placed on them. We not only expect our students to excel academically, but we also expect them to take personal responsibility for their wellbeing by practising 'self-care'. Yes, self-care is important. But where to start? Well, it starts with knowing who that 'self' is which you are intending to take care of.

How many of us can answer that question: 'Who am I?' Can you?

Those of us working in education know that this is one of the biggest questions young people face when growing up. We cannot expect students to 'manage their wellbeing' if they are still discovering who they are and are having to experience all this in schools that are fixated on performance outcomes.

While teachers are busily trying to get students to pass exams, they are struggling with the big questions:

Who am I in the world?
Who am I to my friends?
Who am I to my family?
Who am I going to be?
What kind of impact will I have?

Schools cannot answer these questions for every individual within them. But they can become safe havens, communities in which wellbeing is fostered, identities are safeguarded and young people (and teachers) have a secure environment within which to develop as individuals.

Why is it then, when it comes to the single biggest question that young people face (Who am I?), that schools often (1) fail to encourage students to explore their identities in relationship to themselves, to others and to their work, and (2) fail to acknowledge their identities or even encourage them to separate their learning from their identities? Rather than laying the responsibility for this solely at the feet of educators, perhaps this failure lies also in the curricula that they have inherited, that have been designed without this in mind.

Because this is the reality of any school which is not embracing Total Inclusivity. If one person in your school is not safe, then no one in your school is safe. If one identity is not validated, then no identities are validated.

If we don't encourage students to explore their own identities in a safe and secure community where every individual is respected, how can we challenge perceptions about race or gender? How can we expect students to understand and accept their sexuality, if all they are taught about sex is how it 'works' from a biological perspective? How can we expect students to truly accept themselves and others if nothing they learn speaks to who they are and what they aspire for the world to be?

What we want is for them to aspire for the world to be Totally Inclusive. And this can only truly start with a Totally Inclusive School. That means a school that recognises, values, protects and nurtures a person's authentic intersectional identity.

Total Inclusivity is both an underpinning philosophy of the work that we do and practise. It should inform how we teach and how we work with each other. It should be a school's guiding principle, not a rhetorical statement designed to make the school look good.

We know there are a great many teachers who recognise this and who are working in schools around the world to bring it about. If you are one of them, know that you are not alone.

THE EDUCATOR

We are all students, and we are all teachers, and we never stop being both of these no matter how old we get.

For those of us who have made being an educator our career, by becoming a professional teacher, lecturer or principal, this is an identity which you can never fully let go of, not least because it never fully lets go of you. Once a teacher, always a teacher. Once an educator, always an educator. This is not just a professional identity; it is also a way of being in the world.

That is both a wonder and a challenge. The wonder is in being able to put something back into society, to see students grow knowledgeable, confident and develop as individuals. The challenge is in making sure that influence is appropriate, positive and beneficial for the person on the receiving end of it.

As an educator, we imagine you'll have often worried about how good you are at the job, how effective your teaching is, whether you are helping or hindering the progress of your students, if you are doing more harm than good. The ability to demonstrate this reflectivity is an essential component of effective teaching. If you do not ask yourself these important questions, how can you ask them of your students? If you do not critically reflect on who you are, how can you expect your students to do so?

If you are a school leader or manager, those questions should always be at the back of your mind because you have more of something than almost everyone else in your school: power. How you use that power not only says a lot about you as a leader and as an individual, but it will also largely determine whether your school is an organisation fixated on results or a community of learning. Identities are not protected and nurtured in organisations but in communities.

Total Inclusivity requires each of us to look first at ourselves before we look at others. No educator can stand up and say they never got it wrong, never made a bad judgement, never made an unfair or inaccurate assessment and never contributed, unwittingly or not, to problems of discrimination and inequity in schools.

But we have arrived at a point in human history when ignorance is neither blissful nor permissible. Schools are the first and last line of defence against a society which is, at its worst, abusive, violent and discriminatory. That is the ultimate challenge facing educators – not just to teach maths, science, humanities and languages but to also create a learning environment which protects, nurtures and respects everyone in it.

This book doesn't provide you with every possible solution to every possible dilemma regarding diversity, equity, inclusivity and justice in schools and society. But it does lay out the foundations for getting there. It will help you and your colleagues recognise not just the vital role you play in society but also the enormous influence you have over children and other adults.

THE BOOK

The core structure of the book is based around three sections: You, Us, Institution.

Section One – Total Inclusivity and You

Section One introduces the reader to the key terms and concepts which must be understood when seeking to become a Totally Inclusive School. Following this chapter's introduction to the concept of Total Inclusivity, Chapter Two grounds the idea of Total Inclusivity within the broader concepts of identity, diversity and intersectionality. Here we examine race and ethnicity, sex, gender and sexual orientation and disability. Chapter Three builds on this by taking the reader on a deep dive into understanding what is meant by the terms *implicit bias*, *stereotypes* and *prejudice* and how these beliefs and feelings impact our behaviours and sense of belonging both in our schools and in the wider world. Chapter Four explores the current educational context and our positionality within the existing system. Here, we redefine the purpose of education and examine our role as educators in achieving this purpose and the mindsets and behaviours that will help us create a Totally Inclusive School.

Section Two – Total Inclusivity and Us

Section Two looks at our interactions with others, and issues of respect, dignity and safeguarding. Our identities don't exist in a vacuum. Rather, they are informed by and shaped by the people and groups around us. This part of the book demonstrates how our interactions with others are vitally important in ensuring people feel safe, valued and secure in schools.

Chapter Five examines language and microaggressions. We look at how seemingly innocuous comments accumulate to become barriers to Total Inclusivity, undermining dignity, respect and security of the individual. Chapter Six emphasises the importance of Totally Inclusive systems and policies to ensure that child protection and safeguarding are guaranteed for the whole school community – with all children made safe, not least in their sense of who they are and who they can be. Chapter Seven demonstrates how the valuing of identity and well-being can be used to create Totally Inclusive spaces and outlines how to have courageous conversations about inclusion in your school. The final chapter in this section, Chapter Eight, turns our attention to leadership and leading from where you are, authenticity, overcoming resistance and the impact leaders have when they leverage their positionality and the human resources that will help us achieve our purposes.

Section Three – Total Inclusivity and Your Institution

Section Three provides you, the reader, with a roadmap for guiding your school towards Total Inclusivity. Chapter Nine introduces our Total Inclusivity Continuum and outlines our criteria descriptors against which schools can self-assess their Total Inclusivity growth. Chapter Ten then enables the reader to envisage the larger picture of creating equitable landscapes in their schools. The final section of this chapter takes us back to a core aim of this book which is the need for the individual (you) to become an advocate for Total Inclusivity – the agent of change, who, working in collaboration with community members, can help bring about the Totally Inclusive culture in your school.

BEING REFLECTIVE

We stress the importance of reflectivity throughout the book. This is because reflectivity is an essential element of emotional intelligence. It fosters empathy, understanding and self-awareness.

Yet while we recognise that reflectiveness is important, it is a skill which benefits from some conscious development. If we wish to change in a self-aware, positive way then we need to develop critical, constructive and creative thinking, and that entails being reflective.

This book is not intended to teach you how to be reflective, but it is important to realise that this skill is a central aspect of becoming aware of, and supportive of, Total Inclusivity.

So here is our recommended (and short) learning process towards developing reflectivity in your approach to life; we call this the 'Nine Rs of Reflectivity':

1. Recall a powerful situation, experience, event, encounter you have had or simply something you read or saw, which stirred up strong emotions. Perhaps a relationship breakup, a family fall-out, a toxic encounter at work.
2. Remember the feelings you had, the types of emotions you experienced.
3. Recollect how long it took you to get over those emotions and how they dominated your thoughts and life at the time.
4. Re-examine why the emotions took so long to let go of, and consider how you now feel about that particular situation.
5. Recognise what you learned from that situation at the time, and what you've since learned from it.
6. Regulate your reactions and respond to situations with conscious intention and without ego.
7. Reframe assumptions by considering multiple perspectives and entering spaces with the intent to learn, adapt and treat each individual with dignity.
8. Reflect on how you would now hope to behave should a similar situation or event occur in your life. Would you react the same way or hope not to? The choice is yours to make but it starts with looking back at yourself, and your reactions, in a more critical, less emotional, more constructive and creative way.
9. Realise that to be the person you can be you must first see the person you are.

CHAPTER ONE: REFLECTIONS, GUIDANCE AND COMMITMENT

Reflection Exercise: What does Total Inclusivity mean to you as an educator? Where can you see it operating in your life as a core value system? And when have you advocated for Total Inclusivity?

Guidance for Implementation: Look critically at your current workplace, presumably a school. How Totally Inclusive is it? What barriers are raised against Total Inclusivity? Identify those barriers and start to think about how you can overcome them. This book will help. If you still don't see the importance of Total Inclusivity, then consider those times when you've felt or witnessed injustice. How did this make you feel? Keep these thoughts in mind as we move through each chapter.

Commitment: Total Inclusivity will only come about because of action. Start to think about how important that is to you and how you will make positive change in your own context.

REFERENCES

Aow, A. (2021). Identity, intersectionality and inclusivity. *LinkedIn.* www.linkedin.com/pulse/identity-intersectionality-inclusivity-angeline-aow-she-her-/.

Ball, S. J. (2003). 'The teacher's soul and the terrors of performativity', *Journal of Education Policy,* 18(2), 215–228.

Cambridge University Press. (2022). Community. Cambridge Dictionary. https://dictionary.cambridge.org/dictionary/english/community

Dent, M. & Whitehead, S. (eds) (2001). *Managing Professional Identities: knowledge, performativity and the 'new' professional.* London: Routledge.

Hall, R. (2021). Extreme views and conspiracism rising among England's pupils, research finds. *The Guardian.* www.theguardian.com/education/2021/sep/07/extreme-views-and-conspiracism-rising-among-englands-pupils-research-finds.

Whitehead, S. (2022). *Total Inclusivity at Work.* London: Routledge.

Identity, Diversity and Intersectionality
Chapter Two

Understanding the concept of identity, and respecting this fully, is essential to becoming a Totally Inclusive School. This chapter provides a brief contextualisation of diversity and identity and an overview of different identities (race and ethnicity, sex, gender and sexual orientation and disability), and we outline the importance of taking an intersectional lens when it comes to discussions and understandings of identity. But first of all, we outline what we mean by identity and the different types of identity that we assume.

IDENTITY

The truth is that navigating learning about identity is no easy task. A search for a definition and explanation of identity will yield an endless list of blogs, books and research articles relating to different interpretations of the word, as well as a number of sociological and psychological theories. No wonder, then, that there are academics that dedicate their lives to making sense of this concept!

To put it simply, identity is concerned with "the human capacity … to know 'who's who' and 'what's what'". As Jenkins (2008, p. 5) explains, this involves "knowing who we are, knowing who others are, them knowing who we are, us knowing who they think we are, and so on". It is also concerned with the classification and mapping of the world and our place in it.

Take a minute to consider how you first introduce yourself when meeting someone new. Aside from your name, what is the first thing that you tell them about yourself? Your response to this question will probably give you some interesting insights into how you see yourself and what part of your identity you choose to push to the forefront in a given context.

Some of the things that might come to mind could include your job, where you're from or your key relationships (I am a mother, I am

DOI: 10.4324/9781003231233-3

a husband, etc.). According to Canadian sociologist Erving Goffman (1986), there are three main types of identity: personal identity, social identity and ego identity. For the purpose of this book, we focus on the first two types of identity.

Personal identity is what makes a person an individual in society. It is concerned with a person's biography – the things that make us … us. Our name, place of birth, our roles (mother, daughter, employee, teacher) and our unique personality characteristics (introverted, outgoing, studious, etc.; Clarke, 2008).

However, the aspect of identity which is key to discussions around diversity and inclusion is that of 'social identity', which includes things such as race, ethnicity, gender, sexual orientation and disability. Goffman theorised that society characterises people through identifying certain attributes that we associate as 'normal' within that group. When we meet a stranger, we often make assumptions about the nature of what that person is like and assign them what Goffman terms a 'virtual social identity'. Issues begin to occur when there is a discrepancy between someone's actual social identity and the virtual social identity that we have conjured up in our minds. This is particularly true when this discrepancy relates to some sort of shortcoming that we perceive that person to have. When our (incorrect) perceptions lead us to become prejudiced towards people belonging to particular social groupings including those based on race, gender, sexual orientation and disability, we are now actively discriminating against them (Clarke, 2008; Smith, 2006).

As Vignoles (2018) notes, we have intuitively come to quite like this binary distinction between personal and social identity, particularly those of us that subscribe to Westernised thinking which sees "individuality and sociality as opposing forces" (p. 290). However, on closer inspection, the differentiation between the personal and social aspects of our identities becomes less clear-cut. Depending on the social (and political) context we are in, we may face very different treatment and challenges. But why?

The classifications of social identities are almost never done in a neutral and objective manner and are almost always organised hierarchically. Many aspects of our identity are ranked based on both the way in which these parts of our identity interact with our wider environment and the particular context in which we are examining them.

For example, consider two individual people, one of whom (Person 1) belongs to category 'A' (e.g. male), and the other (Person 2) who belongs to category 'B' (e.g. female). They also both belong to category 'C' (e.g. Principal). Person 1 could be seen as belonging to category 'A' in one context, and category 'C' in another. Depending on how they are categorised by others at any given time, they may be treated differently (more or less favourably) because of this (more on the intersectionality of identities later in this chapter). For example, a parent assumes upon meeting the female principal that she is a classroom teacher and not, in fact, a member of senior leadership (Jenkins, 2008).

Whilst this is a huge simplification, it highlights that identities are interactional and have to be placed in a social context. We know that the human race has always historically ranked identities hierarchically and that this has been done most heavily by the dominant groups in society. Why? To maintain the status quo and, with it, their dominance.

In this respect, it is undeniable that schools are absolutely key in how we all come to see ourselves. School impacts how we view our strengths and weaknesses, our achievements and our hopes and dreams. Educational institutions should strive to provide an environment in which students can recognise, learn about, and evolve their identities. This will lay the foundation for not only what they will learn but also what they will be able to do.

DIVERSITY

If you look at the websites of any educational organisations or institutions (particularly regulatory bodies and universities), you will likely find dedicated webpages that contain any number of the following terms: diversity, equity, and inclusion (DEI). DEI in the UK and DEIJ in the US ('J' represents justice) are particularly popular combinations. Whilst such sites may vary in terms of the depth and breadth of information available, some of the more comprehensive pages will include a pledge or commitment to DEI, alongside DEI and anti-racism resources, campaigns, policies and reports. Despite the availability of such resources, however, what is sometimes more difficult to find is a clear definition of what is actually meant by DEI.

Diversity "refers to individual and group/social differences. These include, but are not limited to, psychological, physical, and social differences that occur among any and all individuals, such as race, ethnicity, nationality, religion, economic class, age, gender, sexual orientation, mental and physical ability. A diverse group, community or organization is one in which a variety of social and cultural characteristics exist" (Quinsigamond Community College, 2022, adapted from Clayton-Pedersen, O'Neill and McTighe Musil, 2013).

Equity, on the other hand, refers to the "practice of ensuring that personal or social circumstances, such as protected class or intersecting identities, are not obstacles to achieving one's potential. Equity is the process an organization engages in to ensure that workplace culture, policies and procedures acknowledge that not all members are afforded the same resources, treatment, and opportunities, and by which the organization works to remedy inequities" (Quinsigamond Community College, 2022, adapted from OECD, 2012).

The third term which is important to understand is *inclusion*, which means that everyone is included, visible, heard and considered. Inclusion is an active and ongoing process of intentional engagement with all members of our learning community to increase diversity, equity and anti-racism (adapted from Clayton-Pedersen, O'Neill and McTighe Musil, 2013). Inclusion in particular should be considered a key concept when it comes to building not merely a school but also a community. When you bring together a wide range of staff and students with different intersectional identities and life experiences, it is crucial that everyone feels a sense of belonging and inclusion.

As Lily Zheng, a DEI strategist and consultant, outlines, "Diversity is an outcome. Inclusion is an outcome. Equity is an outcome." As a school you either have a diverse staff or you don't. Either you have provided everyone with the resources that they need to be successful or you haven't. You either have created an environment in which all identities feel valued and empowered, or you haven't (Zheng, 2022).

This fact requires school leaders to realise that diversity is not a rhetorical device to be deployed on social media platforms as part of a marketing strategy. Diversity must be signified and actualised in school practice.

If a school is not embracing diversity in its staff, then it cannot claim to be a community of diverse identities. If every teacher in a school is white, Western and from a middle-class background and most of the senior staff are cisgender males and heterosexuals, then it is not a healthy school to study or work in. It is a learning community where the power and authority lie with a dominant group, and the lack of diverse representation sends a message to anyone not part of that group that you are not the 'norm' and that you are an 'other' by default.

If some identities (e.g. LGBTQ+) in the school are rendered invisible and silenced not least because everyone is afraid to openly talk about them or acknowledge they even exist, then what kind of learning community is that?

If students (and staff) are not challenged on homophobic language and attitudes or taught how to empathise and interact with those from different cultural and racial backgrounds, then what chance is there for those same students to contribute to society in a safe, productive and harmonious way when they are adults?

We have the minds and hearts of the next generation in our classrooms, in our playgrounds, in our schools. What information are we giving them? What our students experience, encounter and learn goes far beyond the set curriculum. What children experience in your school may shape who they become in the future.

So how can teachers leverage their power to become advocates for Total Inclusivity? Initially, by better understanding the key definitions and concepts relating to race and ethnicity, sex, gender and sexual orientation, disability and intersectionality.

RACE AND ETHNICITY

Race is a complex and often misunderstood term, and one reason for this is that it lacks a clear definition (Smidt, 2020). The term has vague origins, although it is understood to have been derived from early attempts to categorise people based on physical similarities and differences, for example biological markers such as skin colour, bone structure, hair type and colour, eye colour, height and other facial and visible features. However, it is important to note that none of these categorisations has ever been based on scientific evidence. This leads us to the inevitable recognition that race is a social, rather than a biological, construct (Kara, 2020).

'The "social construction" thesis [as related to Critical Race Theory] holds that race and races are products of social thought and relations. Not objective, inherent, or fixed, they correspond to no biological or genetic reality; rather, races are categories that society invents, manipulates and retires when convenient' (Delgado and Stefancic, 2012, p. 8).

Ethnicity, on the other hand, is a term that describes the cultural identity of groups of people and is based on factors such as nationality, ancestry, language, religion and regional culture. So whilst 'race' has historically been determined by how you look, ethnicity is defined by the social and cultural groups that you belong to. Consequently, it is possible to have more than one ethnicity but only one race (Benson and Fiarman, 2019).

For teachers to recognise and accept that their students (and themselves) have many intersecting identities, all of which are influenced to varying degrees by social perceptions and experiences, is fundamental to Total Inclusivity.

We must develop our understanding of the power relations which exist in different identities and in different social/cultural environments; the intersectional nature of identity and the ways in which certain identities (i.e. white) become normalised, resulting in the marginalisation of Black, Indigenous (and) People of Colour (BIPOC).

It is equally unacceptable for educators to claim 'colour blindness' – this is just another way of saying that you don't recognise the entrenched racism operating in society:

[C]olor-blindness asserts that race is no longer a significant factor in social life. In this framework, people, in particular Whites, claim that they "don't see race".... As such, other factors become the drivers of social outcomes, like social class, personal values and motivation, or the economy. What color-blindness actually achieves is the maintenance of White privilege, via its negation of racial inequality and discrimination.

(Cox, 2021, p. 4)

SEX, GENDER AND SEXUAL ORIENTATION

Gender, sex and sexuality are much more complex concepts than first appear. Expectations associated with gender vary dramatically between cultures and are also shaped by societal expectations, including social and legal status. Gender must be considered a spectrum, one that does not conform to the historical boy/girl, man/woman distinctions.

Before exploring gender in more detail, we must also outline the notion of sex or anatomical sex. These terms relate to whether one is assigned as 'male' or 'female' at birth, depending on the physical sexual characteristics that you were born with and develop, including anatomy, chromosomes and hormones. Such characteristics have long been deemed by society as objectively measurable, and this has historically been done in an extremely reductive way. In reality, biological sex is more nuanced. For example, those who are 'intersex' do not fit the binary of the 'male' or 'female' body and can present in a variety of different ways. The number of people born with intersex characteristics and therefore not conforming to the reductivist categories mentioned is much more prevalent than one might imagine, with 1 in 100 births differing from the 'male'/'female' classification (Killermann, 2015).

As a teacher, you might have divided your class into male and female groupings. Whilst this may traditionally have been viewed as an acceptable class management technique, to carry out such practice now is to willfully ignore that there will be students in your schools and your classes whose identities do not fall into either one of these categories.

When we look at gender identity, the complexities grow further.

Dellenty (2019, p. 62) states that gender identity 'relates to one's core sense of self as female or male, or perhaps as having elements of both male and female, or possibly neither (agender)'. Gender identity is concerned with how you think of yourself, and whether you feel that you fit into what society has historically deemed to be the role of 'man' or 'woman'. In this sense, there may be aspects of your identity that align with both, or you may, in fact, find that actually you don't identify with any gender identity. It has generally been widely accepted that we form our gender identities around the age of 3, and this is impacted by our biological sex, as well as our hormones and environment (Killermann, 2015). Gender identity is very personal to us, and so people will differ in the use of terms and labels, depending on what individuals align themselves with:

- Transgender – "An overarching term describing individuals whose gender is not the same as, or does not align with, the *sex* they were assigned at birth."

- Cisgender – "A person whose gender identity is the same as the sex they were assigned at birth or a person whose assigned-at-birth gender identity aligns with their gender identity."
- Transsexual – "A more outdated term for transgender with roots in the field of medicine; can cause offence."
- Non-binary – "A spectrum of identities for people whose gender identity doesn't sit comfortably with either 'male' or 'female'."

(Dellenty, 2019, pp. 236–238)

Another important concept to understand when it comes to discussing gender is gender expression. Gender expression is about "how you demonstrate gender through the ways you act, dress, behave, and interact – whether that is intentional or unintended…. Gender expression is interpreted by others based on traditional gender norms (e.g., men wear pants; women wear dresses)" (Killermann, 2015, p. 4). How an individual expresses their gender can change from day to day and in different contexts. Gender is a spectrum, and gender expression can be motivated by your sexuality, gender identity or how you feel on any given day (Killermann, 2017).

Gender is a core identity for humans, but it is not fixed in biology. Rather, it reflects social and cultural values, norms, attitudes and expectations. Gender must be considered a spectrum, one that does not conform to the historical boy/girl, man/woman distinctions.

Whilst often discussed alongside gender, sexual orientation is quite a separate concept. It is concerned with who you are attracted to emotionally, romantically and sexually and who you may want to have relationships with (Dellenty, 2019). The main labels that you will come across (as they are outlined in discrimination laws) follow:

- Lesbian – "A female who is romantically and sexually attracted to other females."
- Gay – "[O]ften used to describe a man who has an emotional, romantic and/or sexual orientation towards men. Also deployed as a term for lesbian sexuality; some women define themselves as 'gay' rather than 'lesbian'."
- Bi – "Bi is an umbrella term used to describe an emotional, romantic and/or sexual orientation towards more than one gender. Bi

individuals might also describe themselves as **bisexual, pan, bi-curious** or **queer**."

- Heterosexual – "Romantic and/or sexual attraction or behaviour between people of the opposite sex or gender. Sometimes referred to as being **straight**, a term that can offend LGBT+ people as it reinforces heteronormativity."

(Dellenty, 2019, pp. 236–238)

In addition to these four primary labels, there are a number of other labels that might be used by people, depending on what fits them best:

- Queer – This is a term that has historically been used in a derogatory and offensive manner towards gay people. More recently this term has been reclaimed by some of the LGBTQ+ community.
- Pansexual (Pan) – "A person who is sexually attracted to people of any gender."
- Asexual (ACE) – "A person who does not usually feel sexual attraction or urges towards other people. Asexuality exists as a spectrum with variation in levels of romantic and sexual attraction, including a lack of attraction."

(Dellenty, 2019, pp. 236–238)

DISABILITY

According to the UK Equality Act 2010, 'disability' is defined as "a physical or mental impairment that has a 'substantial' and 'long-term' negative effect on your ability to do normal daily activities" (this definition includes autism spectrum disorder and attention-deficit/hyperactivity disorder, specific learning difficulties such as dyspraxia and dyslexia and some mental health conditions if they meet the set criteria; Gov.UK, 2021). Whilst this provides a starting point to understand what is meant by *disability*, as disability rights advocate Emily Ladau (2021) explains, centring definitions of disability purely on what a person can and cannot do focuses definitions around 'inability', and it is important to think much bigger than this. She writes that "it's important to remember that if you've met one disabled person, you've met *one* disabled person" (Ladau, 2021, p. 5). As reported in Ladau's book, disability is more than a perception of 'inability', it is evolving, it is a social identity and it is a lived experience that is inclusive of the barriers and challenges that are placed on an individual because of their diagnosis. One can assume that a person is 'disabled' because of a condition that inhibits their ability to access the world (i.e. the medical model of disability) or one can look at the world as being 'inaccessible' (i.e. the social model of disability) and work to remove the barriers preventing disabled people from fully accessing society.

In relation to this, it is important to understand what is meant by ableism. Ableism can be used "to describe a way of thinking produced through able-bodied experience" (Graham et al., 2020, p. 2). Ableism is highly problematic as it automatically takes the viewpoint that able-bodiedness is the 'norm', and decisions are made with this assumption at the centre. Ableist attitudes include the tendency of non-disabled people to look at disability as something to be pitied, categorising them as 'other' or making assumptions about their ability to do something, or failing to provide appropriate accommodations to support the inclusion of disabled people (e.g. wheelchair ramps, subtitles or sign-language interpreters at presentations, accessible toilets, etc.).

Because of the complexity in the diverse range of experiences and definitions of disability, it is important to recognise that there isn't one way to think about it. But it is important to explore the language we use when we think and talk about disability, as this ultimately serves to shape our understanding. There are two ways of referring to disability: person-first language (PFL) and identity-first language (IFL). PFL highlights the importance of putting the 'person' first, before disability, and this is to emphasise that a disability is something that someone has, and not who they are. Using this language you may describe disability as "a person with Down Syndrome" or a "person with a visual impairment". IFL, on the other hand, refers to using language that recognises that disability is part of someone's identity and part of what makes someone who they are. Using IFL, you might say "autistic person" or "disabled person". Ladau (2021, p. 11) explains that when using IFL, "disability isn't just a description or diagnosis; it's an identity that connects people to a community, a culture, and a history."

It is important to note that neither form of language is right or wrong, but it is an individual's decision as to which definition resonates with them. PFL has much of its origins in the literature from the 1970s, and at the time, there were wider discussions about putting an individual's strengths and experiences before a disability. However, at the time of writing this book, there has been somewhat of a growing movement towards IFL as IFL "is increasingly endorsed as an expression of positive social identity whereby language historically used to dehumanize and marginalise … is redeployed as a form of empowerment" (Vivanti, 2020, p. 2). Whilst there is currently no consensus on the use of PFL or IFL, there are some important considerations to be aware of. Ladau (2021) explains that many people with intellectual or developmental disabilities often use PFL. This has historical roots in the People First movement, and it is a linguistic reminder to recognise an individual's humanity first and foremost. Within the autistic community, IFL language is often intentionally chosen because autism is a key part of someone's identity. For some other diagnoses, it may not be appropriate to use IFL, as you shouldn't refer to someone "a Down Syndrome person". Ladau (2021) advises using PFL as a default unless corrected by an individual to use IFL and, when possible, to ask people their preferred terminology.

Within schools, we need to be aware of both 'visible' and 'invisible' disabilities and intentionally work to remove any barriers that might prevent our students from receiving an equitable educational experience. We must also consider the accessibility of the environments we are inhabiting, and regularly review the effectiveness of the accommodations or strategies we put in place to ensure that all members of our school community have their needs met. We must also consider the language we use when talking about disability and always centre disabled people. This means learning and taking steps to use the language that these individuals feel best represents how they identify.

INTERSECTIONALITY

There is no such thing as a single-issue struggle because we do not live single-issue lives.

– Lorde (2007)

Since its introduction by Kimberlé Crenshaw in 1989, intersectionality has become a dominant theory within critical race studies and gender studies. She described intersectionality as "a lens through which you can see where power comes and collides, where it interlocks and intersects" (Crenshaw, 2017). In this sense, the discrimination that someone faces may not necessarily be the result of a singular identity characteristic (i.e. gender identity, race, sexual orientation or disability). Intersectionality provides us with a concept that acknowledges that the experiences people face can be shaped by a combination of these different things.

As we have shown, identity is complex, diverse, contingent, multilayered and intersectional. Our identities (both personal and social) are dynamic and changing, and all of us have a number of intersecting identities that affect our experiences of the world. As such, to understand how Total Inclusivity might work, we need to recognise the power dynamics which operate within all these identities and consequently operate within and on us.

CHAPTER TWO: REFLECTIONS, GUIDANCE AND COMMITMENT

Reflection Exercise: How do you identify yourself? Take some time out to reflect on who you are, and which core identities define you. Is it your race, ethnicity, age, sex, sexuality, gender, or religion which most signals your sense of self? Was it easy or difficult for you to identify the multiple intersecting identities you hold? Considering your self-perception of identity, are you ever misidentified by others? If so, how so? If not, why not?

Guidance: As Bhopal (2020, p. 808) explains, when intersectionality is used correctly, it is "a useful approach to analyse how overlapping or competing identities affect the experiences of individuals in society".

Therefore, when it comes to working towards Total Inclusivity, any understanding of the problems that our staff, students, or school community face, cannot be fully considered without an intersectional understanding of the issue at play. In the words of Crenshaw:

If we aren't intersectional, some of us, the most vulnerable, are going to fall through the cracks.

(Crenshaw as cited in Moreland-Capuia, 2019, p. 43)

Here, therefore, are some important questions to hold in mind:

- Are my actions promoting intersectional equity or perpetuating inequity?
- Am I part of upholding a singular cultural norm or part of recognising and valuing intersectionalities?
- What can I do to ensure I am valuing and supporting intersecting identities?

Commitment: Once you have fully absorbed and accepted the central tenets of this chapter, consider the next steps you can take within your own schools. Here are some suggestions:

- Commit to your authentic self and safely show up in your school community (where possible and desired) without leaving your identity at the door. It is important to acknowledge here that doing this could pose a personal and/or professional risk, and you, the reader; your colleagues; or your students may or may not have the privilege and/or safety to bring your full and authentic self to school. This is the change we are committing to as part of the Total Inclusivity journey.
- Teachers: Commit to learning more about your students', colleagues', and families' identities and how this intersection of information can inform learning and teaching design.
- Leaders: Commit to establishing infrastructures that collect pertinent information about students to help inform decision-making that impacts how the identities within the school are serviced

REFERENCES

Benson, T. A., & Fiarman, S. E. (2019). *Unconscious Bias in Schools: A Developmental Approach to Exploring Race and Racism*. Cambridge, MA: Harvard Education Press.

Bhopal, K. (2020). Confronting White privilege: the importance of intersectionality in the sociology of education, *British Journal of Sociology of Education*, 41(6), 807–816.

Clarke, S. (2008). Culture and identity. In T. Bennett & J. Frow (ed.) *The SAGE Handbook of Cultural Analysis*, London: SAGE Publications Ltd.

Clayton-Pedersen, A.R., O'Neill, N., & McTighe Musil, C. (2013). Making Excellence Inclusive: A Framework for Embedding Diversity and Inclusion into Colleges and Universities' Academic Excellence Mission. *University of Colorado Boulder*. https://

www.colorado.edu/odece/sites/default/files/attached-files/mei_paper_and_
initiative_briefing_summaries_with_urls.pdf

Cox, J. M. (2021). When color-conscious meets color-blind: Millennials of color and color-blind racism, *Sociological Inquiry*, 1–23.

Crenshaw, L. (2017). Kimberlé Crenshaw on Intersectionality, More than Two Decades Later. *Columbia Law School*. https://www.law.columbia.edu/news/archive/kimberle-crenshaw-intersectionality-more-two-decades-later

Dellenty, S. (2019). *Celebrating Difference: A whole-school approach to LGBT+ inclusion*. London: Bloomsbury.

Delgado, R., & Stefancic, J. (2012). *Critical Race Theory* (2nd ed.). New York: New York University Press.

Goffman, E. (1986). *Stigma: Notes on the Management of Spoiled Identity* (2nd ed.). New York: Simon & Schuster Inc.

Gov.UK (2021). Definition of disability under the Equality Act 2010. *Gov.UK*. https://www.gov.uk/definition-of-disability-under-equality-act-2010

Graham, L. J., Medhurst, M., Tancredi, H., Spandagou, I., & Walton, E. (2020). Fundamental concepts of inclusive education. In L. Graham (ed.) *Inclusive Education for the 21st Century Theory, policy and practice*, Abingdon, Oxon: Routledge.

Jenkins, R. (2008). *Social identity* (3rd ed.). New York: Routledge.

Kara, B. (2020). *A Little Guide for Teachers: Diversity in Schools*. Thousand Oaks: Corwin.

Killermann, S. (2015). Breaking through the binary: Gender explained using continuums. *Genderbread.org*. www.genderbread.org/wp-content/uploads/2017/02/Breaking-through-the-Binary-by-Sam-Killermann.pdf.

Ladau, E. (2021). *Demystifying Disability: What to Know, What to Say, and How to Be an Ally*. New York: Ten Speed Press.

Lorde, A. (2007). "Learning from the 60s" in *Sister Outsider: Essays & Speeches*, eds. Audre Lorde. Berkeley, CA: Crossing Press.

Moreland-Capuia, A. (2019). *Training for Change: Transforming Systems to be Trauma-informed, Culturally Responsive, and Neuroscientifically Focused*. Switzerland: Springer.

OECD. (2012). Equity and Quality in Education: Supporting Disadvantaged Students and Schools. *OECD Publishing*. https://www.oecd.org/education/school/50293148.pdf

Quinsigamond Community College. (2022). Glossary of Diversity Terms. *Quinsigamond Community College*. https://www.qcc.edu/virtual-multicultural-center/glossary-diversity-terms#:~:text=Diversity%20refers%20to%20individual%20and,orientation%2C%20mental%20and%20physical%20ability

Smidt, S. (2020). *Creating an Anti-Racist Culture in the Early Years: An Essential Guide for Practitioners*. Abingdon, Oxon: Routledge.

Smith, G. (2006). *Erving Goffman*. Abingdon, Oxon: Routledge.

Vignoles, V. L. (2018). Identity: personal AND social. In: K. Deaux and M. Snyder (eds.) *The Oxford Handbook of Personality and Social Psychology* (2nd ed.). New York, Oxford University Press.

Vivanti, G. (2020). Ask the editor: What is the most appropriate way to talk about individuals with a diagnosis of autism? *Journal of Autism and Developmental Disorders*, 50(2):691–693.

Zheng, L. (2022). Diversity is a fact, inclusion is a choice, equity—We can do better than this. [LinkedIn]. *Linkedin*. https://www.linkedin.com/feed/update/urn:li:activity:6914608474047852544/

Implicit Bias, Stereotypes and Prejudice

Chapter Three

So far we've talked about the importance of identity, and we've discussed the theoretical underpinnings that relate to 'identity', 'diversity' and 'intersectionality'. We're hoping that you're still with us on this journey and that the theories explored in Chapters One and Two will set the foundations for this next important discussion on implicit bias, stereotypes and prejudice. Remember Total Inclusivity is a journey, not a destination. Whilst the aim of this book is to help you become Totally Inclusive, it is much like a garden that needs regular tending to and nourishment, requiring you to spot weeds and other pests that pose a threat to the overall health of your garden and its ecosystem.

A beautiful garden is never complete, but the foundation and groundwork are pivotal.

Another part of building a strong foundation relates to a better understanding of what is meant by implicit bias, stereotypes and prejudice. This part requires some deep reflection, because implicit bias is not always easy to recognise in ourselves. We'll come back to this later in the chapter.

IMPLICIT BIAS

In March 2021, many erupted in protest when the Commission on Race and Ethnic Disparities report (2021) was published, along with the headline

"UK not deliberately rigged against ethnic minorities"

Within the outpourings of anger that followed, many pointed to the huge amount of data, evidence and lived experience to support the fact that institutional racism is very much still evident across all sections of British society. It raised the question as to how the writers of the report could get it so wrong. Had they been conditioned not to recognise institutionalised racism, seeing it as normalised behaviour?

DOI: 10.4324/9781003231233-4

Historical acts of racism and the images they conjure up reflect public and intentional acts done with the purpose of doing harm, for example policies, racial slurs and racial violence (Scheurich, 2013). However, it is also essential to recognise covert racism and how it operates. Examples are racist 'jokes' and comments, microaggressions (which we explore in Chapter Five), hiring bias, stereotyping and predicting the potential of people based on their race. An invisible barrier is still a barrier, even if it is more difficult to notice. Instead, privilege acts as an invisible force that helps maintain the status quo.

Implicit bias is a major barrier to social justice and 'one of the reasons for the ever-present instances of discrimination and injustice' in both overt and covert forms (Gullo, Capatosto, and Staats, 2018). The term *implicit bias* was first coined by psychologists Anthony Greenwald and Mahzarin Banaji in 1995 (2013), which can be defined as

[u]nconscious attitudes, reactions, stereotypes, and categories that affect behavior and understanding.

(Poorvu Center for Teaching and Learning, 2021)

This form of bias is called 'implicit' because it takes place in the subconscious or 'implicit mind' and therefore can exist without one being conscious of it. Implicit bias consists of both implicit attitudes and implicit stereotypes. An attitude refers to one's evaluation of something such as a person, place or idea, and implicit attitudes are those positive and negative evaluations that take place at a subconscious level. Stereotypes, on the other hand, refer to the belief that the majority of members of a particular group share the same characteristics, for example women are natural carers and nurturers, Asian students are good at maths and young Black males are likely to be criminal-minded. An explicit stereotype is one that you consciously think about and express. Implicit stereotypes, on the other hand, are ones that are less accessible to our conscious control and include those that we may not even be aware of (Project Implicit, 2011).

Example:

- If someone said to you that we have a new primary school teacher joining, would you automatically assume that it was a woman because of the caring nature of this role?

- If you were told that the school had just hired a new head-teacher, would you assume that this is a man because of the association of males with leadership?

It is important to note a few things about this form of bias: it can refer to both favourable and unfavourable assessments of people belonging to different social groups, it can be activated involuntarily without any real awareness of it taking place, it can underpin feelings and attitudes towards other people based on the groups they share characteristics with (such as race, gender and sexual orientation) and this bias develops over a lifetime both through direct and indirect messaging received about different social groups (NEA Center for Social Justice, 2021).

When we think about implicit bias, it can be helpful to think of an unconscious disconnect between our intentions, what we believe in and our actions. For example, the author of this chapter considered themselves to be extremely passionate about equity and treating others with respect and dignity and on a conscious level felt that this was reflected in their behaviours.

However, upon further examination and reflection, they acknowledged that many of these biases did, in fact, exist within them without them having been aware. This highlighted the need for them to examine their biases and the impact that these were having on their students, colleagues and school. They wanted to live more intentionally and consciously with the values that they held dear. They wanted their actions to match up to their values and beliefs.

We all hold these implicit biases, and no one is immune from them.

If we acknowledge that racism, sexism and homophobia (amongst other discriminatory 'isms') are both some of the biggest challenges continuing to face modern society and remain some of the biggest taboos across the world, you can quickly see why implicit bias (or unconscious bias) is often the elephant in the room or, indeed, the elephant in our schools. It is there, but very few people are brave enough to say so.

People reflexively reject and deflect from conversations that could imply that they (or their actions) may be any of these things, especially when they are consciously pro-diversity, equity and inclusion. There is arguably not a more loaded term than the label of 'racist', particularly in the times that we are living in. But these uncomfortable conversations and self-reflections are essential if we are to move towards an equitable society.

For one of the authors who teaches internationally in a British Curriculum school, something they have found themselves reflecting on more recently is their 'Britishness' and how this aspect of their identity has unknowingly shaped how they see the world. The interesting thing is that this was not always apparent until they began working in an international context. All of a sudden, the names on the register didn't resemble that of any class that they had taught before. There were Thai names, Chinese names, Korean names, Japanese names – names originating from all over the world. They saw these on the left-hand column of the register, panicked and were then relieved to find a second column next to it which outlined Anglicised student nicknames … Jerry, Eric, Cathy, Emily. These fitted more with what this author recognised and could easily remember, having grown up in a very 'white' area of the south-east of England.

Problem solved … right?!

Maybe for that particular educator at that particular time. They didn't know how to pronounce the names in front of them, and the students seemed content with the use of nicknames. Embarrassment avoided, problem averted, and Jerry was a good name to move forward with. For the teacher anyway.

Another of the co-authors of this book speaks of being born to Chinese parents and going through the Anglicisation of her own name. She was named Aow Siew Siew by her parents. Aow was their family name, Siew a generational identifier, and Siew a second personal name. By the time she started primary school in Australia as a Year 4 English as a Second Language student, she had been named Angeline Aow by her family, and on her certificate of Australian Citizenship issued in 1988, she officially became Angeline Siew Siew Aow. The author reflected that at the time she didn't question the need to change her name to fit a society made up mostly of white migrants, as outside of her home and family events, she rarely used her Chinese name. She became Angeline Aow, and later Miss Aow in her first primary school post in a suburb of Sydney. Later, in her first international school posting in China, the author commented that staff were given business cards during orientation week which had English on one side and Chinese on the back. She distinctly remembers administrative staff selecting phonetic representations of staff first names using favourable Chinese characters, but the name chosen for her was not her birth name. As such, as an Australian ex-pat of Chinese descent working in China, the author was almost "reborn" with another Chinese name. Upon reflection, it is clear to the author that her parents adopted an Anglo-sounding name for her because they wanted her to 'fit in', much like the administrator in China wanted to help new staff fit in by giving them a Chinese name. By the time she arrived in China, she had learned to value and hold onto her name and be proud of her identity and so asked the school to change the business cards to say 歐秀秀 (Aow Siew Siew).

What these two examples demonstrate is two sides of the same coin: a white educator demonstrating an implicit bias towards 'white' names and an educator of colour going through a process of Anglicising her name in order to fit in and then reclaiming her name and all the history and personal significance that goes with it.

What these examples also reveal is implicit bias in action: A teacher shows hesitancy towards saying a student's birth name or may even avoid saying it altogether. A student adopts an 'English' name even though school may be the only context in which it is used. What does this tell the student about the value placed on their name (and therefore their associated identity) within wider society?

STEREOTYPES

We know that stereotypes refer to generalised assumptions about group characteristics, but why is this a problem? Well, the interesting aspect is that stereotypes capture an association between a group and a particular attribute that is based on some degree of reality. For example:

Men are leaders

As Greenwald and Banaji (2013) explain, almost every stereotype we can conceive of is 'true' in some way. What these authors suggest is that you can visualise any stereotype and then add the word *some* to the start of any statement:

Some men are leaders

It becomes a moot point debating the accuracy of any stereotype because they are often somewhat true and somewhat false. Some may be more valid than others – that is the example that Greenwald and

Banaji (2013) use is that feminists = female. Whilst there are certainly many male feminists, perhaps this holds more truth than (all) males are leaders.

The issue with stereotypes is that they cause us to judge the characteristics of strangers whom we know nothing about, other than their perceived belonging to a group. That person is Black, that man is gay, that person is Chinese. Without giving it any conscious thought, we will use what we know about the stereotypes associated with these groups as a starting point for our perceptions.

A helpful way to better understand stereotypes is to draw on the 'stereotypes wheel' which was initially developed by the Sioux Lookout Anti-Racism Committee (Restoule, 2013) and has been expanded to fit the context of this book (Figure 3.1).

This stereotypes wheel consists of four quadrants: perception, prejudice, discrimination and rationalisation. The model is depicted as a wheel because it is always turning. We start with the upper right 'perception' quadrant, which refers to the ideas that circulate in society about different groups. These abstract ideas and beliefs about certain groups (stereotypes) show up in our implicit biases. Black people are criminals. Lesbians are angry. Asian people are academic.

Women are emotional. We learn these stories through our upbringing, our socialisation and the media and popular culture.

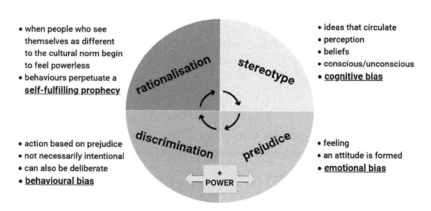

Figure 3.1 Stereotypes Wheel

Sourece: (adapted from Restoule, 2013)

As we start to internalise some of these ideas, we move around the wheel to the next quadrant, 'prejudice', and form an attitude that is based on an idea. This is where the generalisation process takes place, and we start to pre-judge others based on the messages that we have internalised. For example, if a school recruitment panel is looking for a new leader, do they automatically think that a male leader will be best because they have learnt and internalised the idea that men are better leaders? Even those school recruitment panels that are intent on having a diverse senior management team may have internalised the notion that any female appointees need to exhibit characteristics traditionally associated with male leadership (e.g. assertive, forthright, competitive) in order to be an effective leader.

When we allow our prejudicial beliefs to go unchecked, we become discriminatory. Discrimination takes place when we act (or there is action) based on our prejudices. The ideas we have about groups have been internalised and generalised, and we then act either intentionally or unintentionally in a negative way towards a person because of this perception. This is a process of rationalisation, whereby prejudice becomes a 'self-fulfilling prophecy' for the group being discriminated against. People belonging to a particular group may also start to believe that the attitudes and behaviour they experience towards them must be true and, as such, end up having a strong, negative self-belief that causes their behaviours to become self-fulling prophecies. This then creates more evidence to feed into the negative stereotypes and the cycle continues. This becomes more likely to occur when someone experiences such discrimination frequently, for example repeatedly being turned down for a job, repeatedly being put in detention and so on.

To illustrate this using a fairly innocuous example, take the subject of physical education (PE). Imagine a student whose PE teacher believes that a high grade is equated more heavily with physical ability rather than other desirable learning behaviours such as teamwork, sportsmanship, asking questions and effort. If this is the only message that a student receives, they will likely internalise it and believe it to be true. If they are then discriminated against based on this belief, for example they receive poor grades because they are not 'talented' in PE (despite working hard in lessons), this, in turn, becomes a 'self-fulfilling prophecy' in which the mindset of the student shifts to believing that they are indeed a 'failure'. As a result, they decide that they will no longer work hard or put the effort into this subject, because they have internalised the idea that they are not, and cannot, be 'good' at PE. This, in turn, reinforces the PE teacher's beliefs, and decision to discriminate against them, because why would they award a higher grade to a disengaged student who doesn't appear to try? Sound familiar?

It is important to note here that every one of us has the power to interrupt and question our own stereotypical beliefs and prejudices by slowing down our decision-making, reflecting and questioning and adopting objective checks on our processes. Equally, we can interrupt and question biases they see in others' thinking and behaviours, and in the systems, they work in. In doing so, we create an opportunity to 'break the cycle' of negative self-belief caused when individuals or groups repeatedly experience discrimination.

When we move from 'differences' to 'prejudice' we are moving from ideas and beliefs (implicit bias) to something concrete and not only harmful, but dangerous to our school communities (explicit bias). You cannot be a Totally Inclusive School and allow any room for prejudice. It threatens the safety of both students and the wider school community, as it signals that 'you are not welcome here'. Total inclusivity is for everyone, and schools, teachers and leaders cannot undertake this journey half-heartedly. It is no exaggeration to say that your students' lives might just depend on it.

A story disclosed to one of our authors illustrates the importance of weeding out prejudice because, put quite simply, prejudiced educators don't belong in our schools. In this scenario, a student had made the brave step to share with the school administration that they identified as a trans male. This had been a long and painstaking process for the student to not only come to terms with their identity themselves but to also then take the steps to come out to their family, close friends and eventually their teachers and the wider school community. Whilst the teacher who shared this story with us stated that the student and their family had been strongly supported, they commented that one teacher in the staffroom had remarked, "This is ridiculous … I'm not calling her that [name], she's a girl."

If we take this example for a moment and hold the attitude of this educator in our mind (which if we're completely honest, some of us can likely imagine witnessing in our own school contexts) and compare it to the appalling mental health experiences of trans youth, then we can see why making our schools Totally Inclusive is not only important but is also essential. According to the Stonewall Youth Chances Report (2014), which sought to learn about the experiences of LGBTQ+ youth (aged 16–25) in England, 27% of trans young people have attempted to commit suicide, 72% have self-harmed at least once, and 89% of the LGBTQ+ youth that participated in the research have contemplated suicide (as cited in Stonewall, n.d.).

If we return to the example of the teacher who refused to use the student's specified name and pronouns, these words clearly signal that this student is not safe in this space. Why does this matter? Because we cannot have a school where a student is not safe in every classroom, every hallway, and in every interaction.

We as educators will certainly have experienced the rationalisation of these stereotypes by our own students and in interactions between our own students. We may have heard students saying that they like and want to study maths and science because they are Asian or joking that all Asian families want their children to be doctors and engineers. We may have heard students saying that people don't like them because they are Chinese (particularly since the start of the COVID-19 pandemic) or that people assume that they are rude and difficult even before one word has been spoken. We may have heard them express frustration that their teachers often downplay their success because they are Korean and because they believe all Korean students to be hardworking, success is automatically expected of them.

Now let's take that example and extend it to a historically marginalised group in the education system. Is it true that there are more discipline issues related to Black students, or is there an existing stereotype that shapes how behaviour is perceived and/or are there policies in place that disproportionately target historically excluded groups (such as policies regarding dress code)? These stereotypes are ignorant and damaging to individuals and communities and will continue to be unless we challenge the implicit biases at an individual level.

Another area where we see implicit bias and stereotypes play out is in the hiring process. Obiko Pearson (2022) illustrates this point in the context of international schools when she highlights the 'native English speaker' bias and subsequent discrimination. She explains:

> At international schools, a native English speaker isn't someone who aces language proficiency tests. Nor is it a person who comes from any of the more than 50 nations, from Singapore to Nigeria to India, where English is legally an official language and often the de facto tongue of the highly educated. (Globally, such English speakers outnumber speakers from traditionally Anglophone nations by 3 to 1.) Rather, native English speakers are citizens of the U.S., the U.K., Canada, Australia, New Zealand, and Ireland—and sometimes South Africa

Prejudicial attitudes in the hiring practices of schools, and international schools in particular, are pervasive. Many job adverts continue to state a preference for 'native English speakers'. This may sound innocuous enough but, in fact, is a clear declaration about who is welcome to apply and who isn't, as well as exposing a country's racist and classist visa requirements. The use of the term *native speaker* as a required characteristic narrows the hiring pool to those who are most likely Western-educated, have Western passports, and invariably are white, regardless of their English-language proficiency.

One of the co-authors of this book was approached by a former colleague to help recruit for international teaching positions in their school, which was a 'high-tier' international school. Through various connections, job adverts were shared and several applicants submitted their resumes with photos attached. The headteacher ultimately hired a white male applicant whom they described as being 'bang on brand!' In hiring teachers that fit with the 'image' of their elite international school, what they were implying was that white male teachers were the best, and most desirable, candidates based not solely on their teaching ability but on the way they looked and the dominant social groups that they belonged to.

When it comes to examining 'differences' or perceptions, there is always a power dynamic at play between dominant and non-dominant groups. Power can exist in multiple forms, whether that be the ability to make decisions within an organisation or holding social influence in a given context. This may, in turn, be influenced by other factors that come into play, such as the resources you have, your intersecting identities, your personality, your social skills and your connections.

It is also important to note that power shifts back and forth. It can never be truly equal in a relationship, and as educators, we undeniably hold positions of power and influence. Students listen to what we say, observe how we act and react and often model the behaviours and views that we express. Our job is to get curious about the messages that we are perpetuating both consciously and unconsciously, and work to mitigate the discrimination of different groups. Embedding Total Inclusivity as an underpinning philosophy will enable us as educators and leaders to unlearn harmful stereotypes and, in turn, help our students to break free from them.

CONCLUSION

Implicit biases and stereotypes are things that we can no longer ignore or leave untended. They are the weeds in our garden, weeds left to grow and become unruly take the nutrients from the rest of the flowers, and implicit biases and stereotypes take away the richness and goodness of diversity and equity in our schools. What is more, they feed prejudice and prejudice can quickly convert into outright racism, misogyny, homophobia, transphobia and ableism. We might not always notice the weeds growing at first, as we can be busy tending to other areas, but if we fail to look for them then we threaten the life source of our schools. We cannot sit on the fence or be indifferent to prejudice in our schools, nor can we merely accept difference. For flowers to bloom, we must be dedicated to seeing, understanding and valuing all intersectional identities. This will not only make schools better for staff and students now but also for the world to come.

CHAPTER THREE: REFLECTIONS, GUIDANCE AND COMMITMENT

Reflections: Reflect on how you may, in the past, have contributed to the perpetuation of biases and stereotypes regarding different social groups. Perhaps you've done this without realising how those biases and stereotypes had become implanted in your mind. Maybe you failed to realise how you were perpetuating discrimination. Now that you have realised, it's a good time to reflect on how you can avoid this in the future.

Guidance: Implicit bias and stereotypes operate in society and in us all, and have physical, emotional and material consequences for all of us, but especially those on the receiving end of them. Consider completing some of the Harvard Implicit Association Tests (IATs)[1] or other similar assessments, and reflect on your results. What do they tell you about the biases that you hold?

Commitment: Make the commitment to spread the word about implicit bias in your working life – to students, parents and colleagues. Don't stay silent when you see stereotypical thinking at work – raise a voice against it. Remind others about the damage such thinking does to all of us.

NOTE

1 The IAT "measures the strength of associations between concepts (e.g., black people, gay people) and evaluations (e.g., good, bad) or stereotypes (e.g., athletic, clumsy)" in order to measure subconscious/hidden biases. Available at https://implicit.harvard.edu/implicit/takeatest.html.

REFERENCES

Commission on Race and Ethnic Disparities. (2021). Commission on Race and Ethnic Disparities: The Report. Gov.UK. www.assets.publishing.service.gov.uk/government/uploads/system/uploads/attachment_data/file/974507/20210331_-_CRED_Report_-_FINAL_-_Web_Accessible.pdf.

Greenwald, A. G., & Banaji, M. R. (2013). Blindspot: The Hidden Biases of Good People. New York: Delacorte Press.

Gullo, G. L., Capatosto, K., & Staats, C. (2018). Implicit Bias in Schools. New York: Routledge.

NEA Center for Social Justice. (2021). Implicit Bias, Microaggressions, and Stereotypes Resources. NEA Center for Social Justice. www.nea.org/resource/library/implicit-bias-microaggressions-and-stereotypes-resources.

Obiko Pearson, N. (2022). Elite International Schools Have a Racism Problem. Bloomberg. https://www.bloomberg.com/news/features/2022-03-04/elite-international-school-education-runs-on-systemic-racism.

Poorvu Center for Teaching and Learning. (2021). Awareness of Implicit Biases. Yale University. www.poorvucenter.yale.edu/ImplicitBiasAwareness.

Project Implicit. (2011). Frequently Asked Questions. Project Implicit. www.implicit.harvard.edu/implicit/faqs.html.

Restoule, J.-P. (2013). Aboriginal Worldviews Colliding with Newcomers. *Coursera*. www. coursera.org/lecture/aboriginal-education/2-1-4-stereotyping-part-4-16-12-xavCM.

Scheurich, J. J. (2013). *Research method in the Postmodern*. Abingdon, Oxon: Routledge.

Stonewall. (n.d.). Trans Key Stats. Youth Chances Report. *Stonewall*. https://www. stonewall.org.uk/sites/default/files/trans_stats.pdf.

Power, Positionality and Dismantling Inequities

Chapter Four

To round off this first section focused on Total Inclusivity and You, Chapter Four examines our individual position as educators serving in learning ecosystems shaped by social, economic and political systems. To fully understand ourselves, we need to understand the context in which we live and the rules of engagement that exist. We also need to understand how our engagement with cultural norms influences our behaviours and how school systems have evolved. These aspects all play a role in how we show up as educators, and a critical awareness of this makes us conscious of our power,[1] our positionality,[2] our privileges and our complicity in upholding a status quo.

This chapter challenges you to determine how you feel about the current educational context, what you believe we 'owe' our students[3] and how we can co-construct a new educational contract that is Totally Inclusive.

WHAT WE BELIEVE TO BE BROKEN: THE CURRENT EDUCATIONAL CONTRACT

As Angela Y. Davis, an American political activist, famously stated:

> I am no longer accepting the things I cannot change. I am changing the things I cannot accept.

The current educational contract is broken. If we are to become Totally Inclusive, we need to engage in an ethical renewal of the current system, and a rewriting of the educational contract. This process requires us as individuals to identify the principles of our current schooling design that are inequitable. Doing so may not be easy, because we have been conditioned to uphold these cultural norms. And yet, the reality is that these cultural norms, the written and unwritten rules, have not served the diversity of identities that walk through our school doors.

DOI: 10.4324/9781003231233-5

If we want to promote change, we have to cultivate Totally Inclusive mindsets that underpin decision-making and actions. We must identify what is broken and build the change initiatives and interventions we want to advocate for in communal solidarity. To be able to identify our current state and 'what is broken', we need to understand what has gone on before us as these are the systems (within and outside school) that we inherit when we set foot on our campuses. We also need shared understandings of the purpose of education and what we understand a school's role is in achieving this purpose. This is what we mean by the educational contract; the written or spoken agreement regarding the purpose of schools and what it means to be educated.

Universally accepted school structures are normalised as we step out of school systems as students ourselves, then into universities where we learn how to function in schools as teacher trainees, and then back into the school systems as educators, where we continue to uphold the same structures. This trajectory may sound familiar as it is a well-trodden path. For some of you, your time in school was a successful one full of joy and special memories. If you thrived in your own school days, critically reflecting on this structure as one that is inequitable may make you uncomfortable, as your lived experiences are integral to your own professional identity. For others, your time in school may have been one where you experienced marginalisation due to aspect(s) of your identity. If school was a place where you didn't fit in perhaps you entered this profession that caused you harm because you have a strong desire to not let that be another child's experience.

Whatever your entry point may be, we need to get comfortable with the uncomfortable. After all, we are saying that what has been good enough until now is no longer good enough, and that can be a hard thing to accept. A large part of our discomfort lies in our inherent desire to see ourselves as 'good' (Chugh, 2018). We believe that teachers and leaders show up at school with good intentions and a desire to have a positive impact. We also believe that all educators have the power and privilege to create an equitable path. Yet, if all educators have been doing 'good', how is it possible that we are still living in societies, and teaching in schools, where inequities and discrimination still exist and, in some contexts, thrive? Has doing 'good' been good enough?

At the time of writing, the topics of diversity, equity and inclusion in the international school context are being widely discussed by accreditation agencies, school leaders and school staff. As two of the authors of this book work in international schools, this next section draws on this context to illustrate how structural inequities have shaped education across the world.

POWERFUL EDUCATION SHAPERS: THE INTERNATIONAL SCHOOL CONTEXT

The challenge of creating a Totally Inclusive School is a universal one. Education systems around the world have long been underpinned by political ideologies and philosophies, with governments exercising power to use education as a vehicle to promote certain worldviews and values.

International schools originated as a strategic initiative to 'globalise' and offer a national form of education in another country (Hayden and Thompson, 2000). This globalised education effort has historically benefitted expatriate[4] families and was strategically sponsored by national governments and companies looking to attract senior-level corporate executives to serve their economic growth and development. The international school market has seen significant growth from 2,584 international schools educating fewer than 1 million students in 2000 to 12,853 international schools in 2022 serving 5.63 million students (ISC Research, 2022 and Stobie, 2016 as referenced by Larsson, 2021). In January 2022, ISC Research reported that the industry's fee income totals US$53.5 billion. This growth is due to the changing demographics of those attending international schools, shifting from children of ex-patriate, c-level business executives (such as CEOs, CFOs and other senior-level leaders) to the growing middle-class and two-income family units from the school's country base.

According to a Bloomberg article by international school alumni Obiko Pearson (2022), many families believe that Western-style education will provide a clear pathway to success for their children. "Around the world, finishing schools for the Davos class[5] teach excellence – as long as the excellence is White, Western, and English-speaking" (Obiko Pearson, 2022). Obiko Pearson goes on to write that "[p]ower coheres early, and children establish lifelong ties with peers groomed for the global elite." The success and excellence referred to here are tied to economic and cultural capital, and this drives parental decision-making and parental pressure on schools to deliver. Gardner-McTaggart (2020) calls this "social alchemy" and an expectation to turn "ordinary metal of the non-white, non-English student to gold" because "whiteness IS the product". The design perpetuates systems that exclude people with historically marginalised identities whilst simultaneously benefitting those who assimilate into them.

Hayden and Thompson (2008) wrote that

> [n]o country can remain indifferent regarding the way its future elite is being educated, and ... the consequences that international education may have on inequalities, on the national system and its curriculum, on students' access to university, their future professional mobility, and eventually on the country's development.

Whilst international schooling systems serve the global elite and are seen as the gold star model of schooling, they are also often guilty of perpetuating a divide between the 'haves' and 'have-nots'.

The international school context provides the basis for discussions about the need to decolonise the curriculums we teach. The problematic nature of teaching Western, whitewashed curriculums, whilst claiming to nurture 'global' learners is perhaps more apparent in this context, and yet these discussions should not be isolated to the international education system. All schools, wherever they are located, and whomever they teach, must be aware of the biases and injustice that their curriculums so often perpetuate, and engage in dismantling the harmful structures that exist.

DISMANTLING INEQUITY AND DECOLONISING THE CURRICULUM

What is taught in our schools, what counts as 'knowledge' and how we come to know facts and concepts and develop skills, is an issue of power (Young, 1971). As Hughes (2021) says, "curricula do not fall out of the sky, they are designed by people." What is included in curricula, the choices educators make to design learning, is invariably influenced by and a reflection of the geopolitical context in which schools are located. Take a look at most of the scientists and writers who are studied and celebrated in schools. The likelihood is they don't come from the cultures and countries that those schools are located in.

Nor will they represent marginalised groups in society, be they women; LGBTQ+ persons; Black, Indigenous and People of Colour; or disabled people. Can we honestly say that the content we teach and the people that we learn about at school truly reflect the diversity of the society that we live in? The reality is that curricula around the world generally reflect the views held by the dominant culture within your school. Who belongs in the dominant culture varies depending on your school's culture and context. School systems have provided certain identity groups with privileges and power, and it has also created groups of 'others' that do not have the same visibility and access as they sit on the margins.

Calls to decolonise curricula by decentering singular narratives and situating the histories and knowledge that do not originate from the dominant culture are echoing across educational sectors globally. To lift historically marginalised voices to the centre and decolonise is not about deleting knowledge or histories but ensuring that students, educators and community members can be who they are and want to be. It is about situating history and knowledge that does not originate from the context of imperialism, colonialism and power and centring those who have been historically marginalised (Arshad, 2021). For example, the teaching of history is never truly objective, and curricula have long propagated different nationalist and colonial agendas, whether implicitly or explicitly. Many portrayals of the British army during World War I do not address the role of troops from colonised India, which provided 1.2 million men who were deployed (Roychowdhury, 2021). Similarly, portrayals of the American army during World War II have traditionally not addressed the Black Americans who served and faced segregation both at home and on the war front (Clark, 2020).

Curriculum designers have power. Leaders who have a say in the curricular frameworks used in schools have power. And those of us who teach it also have power. We can approach the content of what we teach critically so that our students are exposed to multiple narratives and have the opportunity to think critically and decide for themselves. Educators also need to be aware that what we chose not to teach also sends a message to our students about what we deem to be important enough to spend time learning and what will end up outside our students' scope of learning.

According to Wilkerson (2020, p. 70) in her book *Caste – The Lies That Divide Us*, caste is "the granting or withholding of respect, status, honor, attention, privileges, resources, benefit of the doubt, and human kindness to someone on the basis of their perceived rank or standing in the hierarchy". Wilkerson goes on to describe that caste is powerful because it is not necessarily overt hatred or a personal attack, but it is interwoven into routines, expectations and patterns of a social order that has been in place for so long that it is seen as a natural order of things. This hierarchy deems a dominant social group as worthier than another of respect and dignity.

A casteist person is one who is invested in keeping hierarchies as they are. They are content to do nothing to change it. While caste is not the cause for every poor outcome or unpleasant encounter, it is a factor in interactions and decisions that educators make in schools. For example, consider a traditional school ecosystem in which there is likely to be an organizational chart that outlines a head of school at the top, teachers somewhere towards the bottom and administrative support staff branching out to the side. In such structures voices in decision-making have hierarchical power and players within the system may not always be thinking about students at the forefront of decision-making (since they are often left off an organizational chart). Does this make the voices of students or teachers who interact with them less important in the decision-making process in a school? Think back to a time when a good idea was left hanging because it wasn't an administrator who came up with it. Or when decisions that impact teachers are handed down to be implemented without consultation. This is a caste system at play in which rank or standing is valued more than dignity and worth.

Other ways caste manifests in schools may be seen in the dominance of certain cultures, religions and languages. Consider the messages your school signals to the community through its mission and vision, policies, its calendar of events and what is celebrated. Any identities that function outside of this messaging are seen as 'other' and can be perceived as a challenge, or even a nuisance, to have to deal with rather than truly embracing and valuing cultural, religious and linguistic diversity.

For example, in one class in a school in Germany, families celebrate Christmas, Hannukah, Diwali and Kwanzaa leading up to the end of the calendar year. However, in the school's traditional learning ecosystem, Christmas is seen as the default, and students who are not Christian leave their identities at the classroom door and assimilate into learning engagements from the dominant culture. Meanwhile, when students are absent for religious reasons such as Lunar New Year or Eid, it is seen as an interruption to learning. This is not to say that students cannot learn about Christianity, it is pointing out that by default Christianity is seen as the religion of value that is integrated into decision-making in the schooling system above others.

Language also has power in your school ecosystem. It determines students' access to the curriculum and families' and caregivers' access to information about the school. How a person commands and uses language can either gain them linguistic capital or put them on the outskirts. English-medium schools are prevalent in many non-English-speaking countries and, of course, the language of instruction in countries where English is the national language. As a result of imperialism and colonialism, English-medium schools dominate and so has the concept of being a 'native speaker'. This places power and hierarchy on those who speak a 'Queen's English' or another highly valued accent such as American or Canadian. Meanwhile, across the globe, different Englishes exist, and within a school community, there may be a diversity of English speakers from Malaysia, India, Jamaica, the Philippines, and others. This linguistic power differential manifests in schools in multiple ways, such as when educators applying for jobs are discriminated against due to their ancestry rather than their linguistic competence. Or when students leave parts of their linguistic identity at the door and adopt their school language as one to aspire towards. This results in language loss, and in the worst cases, students enter school as multilinguals and exit as monolinguals.

So how does your school value multilingualism? Does your school conform to the guidance provided by the government your school functions in? Are you aware of the linguistic diversity of your school community? When a child's home language or languages differ(s) from your school's language of instruction are you as an educator, and your school in its infrastructure, designed to foster multilingualism in students? Or is your school one where multilingual students are conditioned to leave their identities at the school gate in order to assimilate to your school's culture? Do they add to their linguistic profiles without losing the languages they enter school with? These questions may be familiar to you if your school is actively addressing this. If these considerations are new to you, it will be worth your while to probe further as you consider how your language of instruction has been prioritised at the expense of home language(s) and what this signifies to historically marginalised individuals in your school community.

A shift we need to make is to consider the opportunities that intercultural, multilingual families bring to our school ecosystems. Imagine if language and different ways of knowing are integrated to make the school a rich place of learning for intercultural understanding. Educators have power in education systems as they influence the design of learning and teaching. We need to examine how we are reinforcing ideas of supremacy and dominant ways of seeing that have reproduced unequal dynamics that undervalue knowledge, ideas and languages from historically marginalised groups (Andreotti and de Souza, 2008).

One of the authors worked from 2000 to 2002, in a middle-class suburban school in western Sydney, Australia, in a government school that served local families. In this school, which was non-secular, weekly assemblies were held where the Lord's Prayer was recited. English was the medium of instruction, with no recognition of the diverse linguistic backgrounds of students entering the school. The cultural context of the school is one rooted in colonialism, and until 2000, all teachers at the school came from white migrant backgrounds. Fast-forward 20 years and changes include acknowledgement of land and country taking place during assembly gatherings and multilingualism being more greatly valued as a fact, right and resource. Decolonising education is starting to permeate educational decision-making, and educators who strive to be Totally Inclusive need to understand deco-loniality as an ongoing undoing of colonisation.

Ways in which educators have shifted colonial narratives and power include:

- Christmas and Easter holidays renamed to summer/winter and spring/autumn holidays.
- discriminatory native English-speaker requirements removed from job descriptions.
- multilingualism being valued through inclusive language policies.

- religious identities of the school population being recognised and celebrated.
- increased representation of historically marginalised identities throughout the curriculum and in media resources.

Colonial underpinnings resulting in class and caste divisions, racism, sexism, heteronormativity, religious othering and linguistic dominance make people who fall outside the dominant social group think less of themselves, making them more vulnerable to discrimination. A Totally Inclusive educator is, at their core, a caring person who treats each human being with dignity. Totally Inclusive educators go beyond tolerance; they value differences and seek to adapt rather than dominate. A Totally Inclusive educator also seeks to utilise their positionality to dismantle hierarchical structures that are founded on prejudice and discrimination. They value multilingualism and understand the iterative relationships between language and culture. Most of all, a Totally Inclusive educator is committed to decolonising education and dismantling casteism.

REDEFINING SCHOOL SUCCESS

To successfully dismantle inequity in schools, educators need to determine what they are teaching for and the power they have, whatever their role and responsibility is, to be Totally Inclusive. To date, our educational systems have prioritised academic performance, nationalistic agendas, compliance and homogeneity. This has come at the expense of nurturing healthy, well-balanced, non-violent, non-aggressive human global citizens. When academic performance is seen as the primary means of gaining economic capital in the future lives of students, we are more likely to make decisions that we think will help them get there. Therefore, to engage in an ethical renewal of schools to become Totally Inclusive places we need to reimagine and redefine what it means for schools to be successful. The answer lies in how you envision a successful graduate and if this aligns with your school's mission and vision.

Johnson (2020) wrote that we need

> [a] different narrative for education; telling our students a different story about what – or who – their education is 'for'. Shifting the emphasis from exam results, and instead using education as a tool for building a

fairer future. Re-shaping our system to be more focused on our young people's own life stories – including their present and future wellbeing.

Ensuring that our students become reflective, equitable and inclusive adults must be the bigger goal here.

CONDUITS FOR CHANGE: CULTIVATING MINDSETS AND GUIDING PRINCIPLES

Identifying inequities is a complex and multilayered pursuit. The more we uncover a topic the more we discover interrelated subtopics worth exploring. In addition to being skilled in our profession as teachers, it is critical to understand that since schools are reflections of social structures, it is vital that we are aware of our stance around key topics, as our beliefs and opinions influence our decision-making in schools.

A single chapter cannot adequately dive into key topics educators need to be aware of. Therefore, we offer an overview of key topics that should be fundamental to educator training courses if we are to build educators' collective capacities, knowledge, conceptual understandings and skills to both recognise inequities and to drive change. Directly related to these key topics are mindsets and guiding principles that educators who are committed to creating a Totally Inclusive School need to cultivate. The mindsets outlined in Table 4.1 are key conduits for change. With these mindsets present in the majority of educators, achieving Total Inclusivity in schools will be accelerated.

Needless to say, learning about the diverse identities in our school communities is at the core of understanding differences and how we can meet these needs as educators. The topics listed in Table 4.1 are starting points and not an exhaustive list. There are also overarching topics that cross over these categories that educators need to know about. Some of these include the following:

- Intersectionality
- Forms of harm, safeguarding and child protection
- Laws related to anti-discrimination, racism, sexual harassment, provision for disabilities, etc.
- Restorative justice practices[6]
- Trauma-informed practices[7]
- Culturally responsive teaching[8]

Table 4.1 Topics All Educators Need to Know and Mindsets of Totally Inclusive Educators

Key Topics All Educators Need to Engage with that Impact Educational Decision-Making	Mindset and Guiding Principles
Gender Inequity and these related concepts: • Sexism and gender biases • Social construct of gender and spectrum of gender identities • Pronoun usage • Masculine and feminine archetypes • Toxic masculinity • Gender and pay leadership gaps • Feminism and intersectionality	To address gender inequity in the patriarchal system that exists today educators need to embrace feminism and be **feminists**. Educator feminists recognise that gender inequity impacts women differently. For women of colour and transgender women, double discrimination is at play. Intersectional approaches are essential.
LGBTQ+ marginalisation and these related concepts: • Heteronormativity, cisnormativity • Homophobia and transphobia • Oversexualisation of LGBTQ+ people • LGBTQ+ allyship • Laws related to LGBTQ+ people	To address homophobia and transphobia educators need to be **LGBTQ+ allies**. An LGBTQ+ ally rejects fear-based assumptions and negative and harmful stereotypes of LGBTQ+ community members. They advocate for and normalise the diverse ways people love and have relationships.
Racism and these related concepts: • Whiteness, white fragility, white privilege and white supremacy • 'Othering' • Class and caste systems • Intercultural understanding • Ethnicity • Ancestry and intergenerational trauma • Citizenship and residency statuses • Migration and transglobal identities • Internalized racism	To address racism educators need to be **antiracists**. Educators need to recognise that everyday racism is prevalent as we are conditioned to think of dominant races as superior and others as inferior. Understanding that reverse racism does not exist and that elevating marginalised races does not diminish the position of the dominant race.

Table 4.1 (cont.)

Key Topics All Educators Need to Engage with that Impact Educational Decision-Making	Mindset and Guiding Principles
Neurodiversity, disabilities and these related concepts: • Neurodiversity, neurodivergent and neurotypical • Autism spectrum, dyspraxia, dyslexia, attention-deficit/hyperactivity, dyscalculia, and others. • Ableism and ableist stereotypes • Learning diversity and inclusive practices • Universal Design for Learning • Accessibility and differentiation	To address ableism educators need to be **anti-ableists**. Anti-ableists actively work to dismantle ableism. Educators who are anti-ableists see it as their responsibility to address the needs of learners under their care. They advocate for accessibility and inclusivity.

A Totally Inclusive educator recognises that one's mindset is not a permanent part of a person's identity and that this can fluctuate and change. They also believe that schools have an important role and responsibility in addressing and eliminating discrimination and understanding that being a Totally Inclusive educator involves critical self-reflection and action (Barbieri and Ferede, 2020).

We need to be feminists, LGBTQ+ allies, anti-racists, neurodiversity advocates and anti-ableists. These are the mindsets of Totally Inclusive educators who will use their positionality to elevate the voices of the traditionally marginalised and have intercultural competency skills to bridge differences.

WHAT WE OWE OUR STUDENTS: A NEW EDUCATIONAL CONTRACT

Jacqueline Woodson and López (2022) wrote in *The Year We Learned to Fly*:

> Sometimes the first step toward change is closing our eyes, taking a breath, and imagining a different way.

To create a Totally Inclusive School, educators need to reimagine. We need a new educational contract that redefines the purpose of education and the school's role in achieving this purpose. We also need to continually develop the individual mindsets, behaviours and infrastructure that will help create sustainable change.

This reimagining begins with recognising that we have not always made decisions that considered all students at the core and heart of what we do. It is a commitment to taking responsibility for the systems we have inherited, because when we know better, we should do better. The ability to envision in liberatory ways without fear and with a 'can do' attitude is essential. Educators need to dismantle the structural inequities that are always working against, holding the historically marginalised back.

Education is a service industry. While it can be big business for some, the business of education is to serve the students in our care. Even in the business world ethical renewals are possible, as can be seen with fair-trade partnerships that seek greater equity in international trading conditions. For example, since 1973, Fair Trade Original in the Netherlands has imported coffee from cooperatives of small farmers in Guatemala and the fair-coffee concept paved a pathway for fair trading across other products like tea, cocoa, sugar and more (World Fair Trade Organization, 2022).

Building on this, let us view coffee as a metaphor for schooling. As educators we have made and consumed multiple cups of coffee and done this routinely. We drink it, enjoy it and have come to rely on it. Sometimes we spill a cup. It was not our intent to do so. We made a mess. We aren't going to leave it there. We clean it up and then perhaps consider investing in a sealable Thermo mug that not only prevents spills but also keeps one's coffee hot for longer. Our current educational systems are not too dissimilar. We have contributed to upholding schooling models that have caused harm to students, yet we routinely brew the same blend and do so regularly. Only when an "accident" happens do we think about cleaning up our spills (e.g. when a serious incident occurs or when alumni publicly vocalise the harm they experienced in our institutions.) We need to take responsibility and consider how to prevent such spills from occurring in future.

We can redesign our schools and create liberated art out of spilled coffee.

We have the individual and collective power to impact our learners, our colleagues and to successfully drive change. Everyone in a school community can contribute by leveraging their situational power to make a difference. To do so take these simple-in-concept and hard-to-take steps:

1. Learn about the needs of the historically underserved in our school communities.
2. Take responsibility for the injustice(s) that have passed.
3. Pave a path for institutional restorative justice (recognition of and taking responsibility for the harm a school has caused to past and present graduates).
4. Co-construct a new practice that liberates and serves all students.

A new educational contract values students who enter our campuses as their diverse, authentic selves. It recognises that schools are key places where our children and youth are learning about and evolving their individual identities. We, the educators, are here to help students discover their diverse identities, provide them with equitable access to the curriculum, find ways to include everyone and lift the historically marginalised in order to achieve justice (Table 4.2).

Shaping the minds of students remains a goal, and in a new educational contract, our learners are also asked to shape their hearts and hands. We will challenge them to discover what kind of impact they want to have in the world. Your new educational contract is waiting for you to uncover in your school community. To redesign school so that it is Totally Inclusive: this is what we owe our students.

CHAPTER FOUR: REFLECTIONS, GUIDANCE AND COMMITMENT

Reflections: At the beginning of this chapter, we asked you to consider how you feel about the current educational context. Reflect further on these questions:

- The perspectives you have been teaching: Has your design of learning and teaching incorporated the diversity of identities your student body is composed of?
- Your school's culture and context: What educational norms have you accepted in the past, and can now no longer accept?
- Your individual 'why' and purpose: How would you define a new educational contract? Does your vision of schooling align with your school's mission and guiding statements?
- Your positionality and power to act: What is within your realm of influence? What do you not have control over that you need to accept in order to move forward? How can you leverage your position, power, privilege and community relationships to enact positive change? What personal actions can you control?

- Your role and responsibility as an educator: Are my actions promoting equity or perpetuating inequity? Am I part of upholding historically inequitable structures or part of empowering the diversity of identities reflected in the school's community? What will I do?

While reflecting on these questions emotions will undoubtedly arise. Feeling shame and guilt, mixed with anger, sadness and fear are common reactions, and this is evidence that you care and want to do better. Reflect on ways to work through those feelings and self-regulate to a point where you are ready to take the next step towards creating a Totally Inclusive School.

Guidance: As educators we are responsible for the learners under our care, for the ways we collaborate with our colleagues and for the interactions we have with the school community as we develop partnerships for learning. These relationships are shaped by cultural norms and characteristics that show up in attitudes and behaviours. The following considerations in (Table 4.2) are offered to help shift away from ways of knowing, thinking and working that have led us to where we are today and towards ways of knowing, thinking and working that will lead us towards a more inclusive, equitable and just future.

Table 4.2 Ways of Knowing, Thinking and Working[9]

Ways of Knowing, Thinking and Working	
Shift Away From	**Shift Towards**
Perfectionism	A culture of appreciation
Sense of Urgency	Realistic work plans and expectations
Defensiveness of existing organisational structures (seeing criticism as a personal threat)	Understanding how defensiveness gets in the way of the mission and supporting yourself and others to avoid taking things personally
Quantity over Quality	Focus on values, processes and quality of goals
Worship of the Written Word	Value multiple communication methods and the messages over the means
Only One Right Way	Value alternate ways (that are not your own) and strive to co-construct ways to achieve a goal

Table 4.2 (cont.)

Ways of Knowing, Thinking and Working	
Shift Away From	**Shift Towards**
Paternalism (decision-making that is clear to those with power and unclear to those without it)	Transparency and understanding of decision-making considerations and processes
Either/or thinking and oversimplification of complex things	Yes/and thinking and managing polarities[10]
Power hoarding	Power sharing
Fear of open conflict (resulting in ignoring, avoiding, deflecting or seeing conflict as rudeness or resistance)	Elevate how to have hard conversations and raise hard issues with a focus on co-constructing resolutions
Individualism (believing that you are responsible for solving problems alone)	Collectivism (working together with others towards shared goals)
I'm the only one (who can get it done)	Share responsibilities / delegate
Progress is bigger, more	Consider the impact of actions in the long-term
Objectivity	Recognise that everybody has ways of knowing, thinking and working and that objective (or rational) thinking devalues emotional, intuitive and non-linear approaches
Right to Comfort	Understand that discomfort is a part of the growth and learning process

The purpose of listing these characteristics as outlined by Okun (n.d.) is to guide you to become more conscious of the unwritten norms that make it difficult for change to occur.

Commitment: As we conclude the first section focused on you, the following commitments will support you to cultivate a mindset that advocates for total inclusivity. We encourage you to commit to:
- being a lifelong learner – We expect this of our students and this same commitment is necessary for educators to learn about the many key concepts mentioned in this chapter, throughout this book, and beyond.

- being the antithesis of the inequity that you recognise – As outlined in this chapter to tackle racism, be an anti-racist; to tackle gender inequity, be a feminist; to tackle ableism, be an anti-ableist; and so on. A commitment to elevating the most marginalised identities is a commitment to creating a better and more equitable future for all people and their diverse identities.
- using your positionality to make a difference – To enact change we need to leverage our relationships with community members. We are all leaders who can use our power, privilege and position to make a positive difference.
- constructing a new educational contract – To deliver what we owe our students, educators need to know their students and together in communal solidarity co-construct ways to serve their needs. Committing to this as an ongoing process of defining and redefining schooling that is contextually relevant (as opposed to going through motions to uphold inequitable norms) is a commitment to total inclusivity.

NOTES

1 When we think about power it often has negative connotations as we associate it with abuse of power, ego and self-aggrandisement (Kise and Watterston, 2019). Having power can be seen as a negative and if anything needs a rebrand it is power. Power is not bad, and we need to learn how to turn power into empowerment (Kise and Watterston, 2019). Using power **with** people and not **over** people to make a difference is expanded on in Chapter Eight about leaders and leading.

2 Positionality refers to one's social identity, standpoint, cultural practices and how one understands and views themselves in relation to the world. It is also one's social, cultural and political location, and the power this position has, in relation to another person in a particular context (IGI Global, n.d.).

3 In Minouche Shafik's book (2021) titled *What We Owe Each Other – A New Social Contract* two key questions are explored: What does society owe each of us? And what do we owe in return? This social contract shapes our human experience in societies. Schools are a reflection of societies and influenced by Shafik this chapter questions the current universally understood school contract and proposes a new paradigm that is needed for educators to create Totally Inclusive institutions.

4 An expatriate (shortened to expat) is a person temporarily or permanently residing in a country other than that of the person's upbringing. The word comes from the Latin terms *ex*, meaning "out of," and *patria*, meaning "country" or "fatherland" (Koutonin, 2015). An immigrant is someone who moves to another country to live permanently and with an intent to gain citizenship in the destination country. There are hierarchical politics between these two terms that relate to migrants. *Expat* and *immigrant* can be interchangeable, and bias leads higher

socio-economic, white, temporary or permanent migrants to be referred to as expats while migrants from the global South and lower economic classes tend to be labelled as immigrants.

5 Every January the World Economic Forum (WEF) invites business and government leaders to the Swiss Alpine resort town, Davos. The global elite represented are known as the 'Davos class'.

6 Restorative justice is an approach that focuses on mediation and agreement rather than punishment, and it focuses on accepting responsibility for harm and making things right with victims (WeAreTeachers Staff, 2021). It is used in schools where the focus is on justice, healing and student growth and development. It can be used to help the historically marginalised.

7 Trauma-informed practices recognise that harm is more common than we realise. Trauma-informed and trauma-sensitive approaches take into consideration events that limit a child's ability to learn, grow and thrive (Crisis Prevention Institute, 2021). It is focused on building resilience and social emotional skills.

8 Culturally responsive teaching is an approach where teachers are critically aware of the sociopolitical context schools operate in and are intrepid in their approach that goes against the status quo (Rucker, 2019). This approach recognises that students need to understand themselves, each other, and the system that is around them in schools and society. Culturally responsive teachers understand that developing relationships with their students based on understanding, respect and dignity is the basis for student achievement.

9 The descriptors of white supremacy culture as described by Okun (n.d.) informs the ways in which we have been conditioned to value certain attitudes, behaviours and working traits and the antidotes to counteract these dominant ways of thinking.

10 Polarities is further described in Chapter 8 about Leaders and Leading.

REFERENCES

Andreotti, V., & de Souza, L. M. T. M. (2008). *Learning To Read the World Through Other Eyes.* Derby, UK: Global Education.

Arshad, R. (2021). Decolonising the curriculum – how do I get started? *Times Higher Education.* https://www.timeshighereducation.com/campus/decolonising-curriculum-how-do-i-get-started

Barbieri, C., & Ferede, M.K. (2020, June 29). A future we can all live with: How education can address and eradicate racism. UNESCO Futures of Education Ideas LAB. https://en.unesco.org/futuresofeducation/ideas-lab/barbieri-ferede-education-eradicate-racism.

Bourdieu, P. (1986). The Forms of Capital. In: Richardson, J. ed., *Handbook of Theory and Research for the Sociology of Education.* Westport, CT: Greenwood.

Chugh, D. (2018). *The Person You Mean To Be: How Good People Fight Bias* (1st ed.). New York, NY: HarperBusiness.

Clark, A. (2020). Black Americans Who Served in WWII Faced Segregation Abroad and at Home. *History.* https://www.history.com/news/black-soldiers-world-war-ii-discrimination

Conceicao, I. (2020, March 9). Reverse racism is coming: The backlash against Race Conscious Politics in contemporary Brazil. OHRH. https://ohrh.law.ox.ac.uk/reverse-racism-is-coming-the-backlash-against-race-conscious-politics-in-contemporary-brazil/

Crisis Prevention Institute. (2021, March 31). *How trauma informed schools help every student succeed: Crisis Prevention Institute (CPI)*. Crisis Prevention Institute. https://www.crisisprevention.com/en-CA/Blog/Trauma-Informed-Schools

Freire, P. (1970). *Pedagogy of the Oppressed*. United Kingdom: Penguin Random House.

Freire, P. (1993). *Pedagogy of the Oppressed*. United Kingdom: Penguin Random House.

Gardner-McTaggart, A. C. (2020). Washing the world in whiteness; international schools' policy. *Journal of Educational Administration and History*, 53(1): 1–20.

Goldstein, D. (2022, March 18). Opponents call it the 'don't say gay' bill. here's what it says. *The New York Times*. https://www.nytimes.com/2022/03/18/us/dont-say-gay-bill-florida.html

Hayden, M., & Thompson, J. (2008). *International Schools: Growth and Influence* (Vol. 92, Ser. Fundamentals of educational planning). UNESCO: International Institute for Educational Planning, Paris. https://unesdoc.unesco.org/ark:/48223/pf0000180396

Hayden, M., & Thompson, J. (2000). Quality in diversity. In: Hayden, M. and Thomson, J., ed. *International Schools and International Education*. London: Kogan.

Hughes, C. (2021). Decolonising the curriculum. Council of International Schools. https://www.cois.org/about-cis/perspectives-blog/blog-post/~board/perspectives-blog/post/decolonising-the-curriculum

Kise, J. A. G., & Watterston, B. K. (2019). *Step in, Step up: Empowering Women for the School Leadership Journey*. Bloomington, IN: Solution Tree Press.

What is white privilege? Racism. No Way! (2020, June 18). https://racismnoway.com.au/about-racism/understanding-racism/white-privilege/

IGI Global. (n.d.). What is positionality. Retrieved March 20, 2022, from https://www.igi-global.com/dictionary/positionality/23040

Johnson, E. (2020, April 2). Why we need feminist schools 1. Be Her Lead. https://www.beherlead.com/why-we-need-feminist-schools-1

Johnston, A. (2003). The British Empire, colonialism, and missionary activity. In *Missionary Writing and Empire, 1800–1860* (Cambridge Studies in Nineteenth-Century Literature and Culture, pp. 13–37). Cambridge: Cambridge University Press. doi:10.1017/CBO9780511550324.002

Kendall, Frances. (2006). *Understanding White Privilege: Creating Pathways to Authentic Relationships Across Race*. Oxon: Routledge.

Kendall, Frances. (2013). *Understanding White Privilege: Creating Pathways to Authentic Relationships Across Race*. Oxon: Routledge.

Kendi, I.X. (2019) *How to be an Antiracist*. New York: One World, Penguin Random House LLC.

Koutonin, M. R. (2015, March 13). Why are white people expats when the rest of us are immigrants? *The Guardian*. https://www.theguardian.com/global-development-professionals-network/2015/mar/13/white-people-expats-immigrants-migration

Larsson, J. (2021, November 11). *The changing landscape of international education: It's time to change our terminology.* Council of International Schools. https://www.cois.org/about-cis/perspectives-blog/blog-post/~board/perspectives-blog/post/the-changing-landscape-of-international-education-its-time-to-change-our-terminology

Obiko Pearson, N. (2022). *Elite International Schools Have a Racism Problem.* Bloomberg.com. https://www.bloomberg.com/news/features/2022-03-04/elite-international-school-education-runs-on-systemic-racism?sref=Umh7YXqB

Okun, T. (n.d.). *"White Supremacy Culture,"* Dismantling Racism Works. www.dismantlingracism.org/uploads/4/3/5/7/43579015/okun_-_white_sup_culture.pdf

Rucker, N. W. (2019, December 10). Getting started with culturally responsive teaching. *Edutopia.* https://www.edutopia.org/article/getting-started-culturally-responsive-teaching

Roychowdhury, A. (2021). 'Discriminated even in death': How Indian soldiers battled racism overseas during World War I. *Indian Express.* https://indianexpress.com/article/research/discriminated-even-in-death-how-indian-soldiers-battled-racism-overseas-during-world-war-i-7295099/

Shafik, N. M. (2021) *What We Owe Each Other – A New Social Contract.* London: The Bodley Head.

Tanu, D. (2018). *Growing up in Transit – The Politics of Belonging at an International School.* New York: Berghahn Books.

Turner, P. (2021) To What Extent Can International Schools Contribute to the Dismantling of Systemic Racism? Perceptions of Teacher-Volunteers in Diversity, Equity, Inclusion and Justice Working Groups in 'Pioneer' International Schools. Bath, University of Bath.

WeAreTeachers Staff. (2021, July 27). What teachers need to know about restorative justice. We Are Teachers. https://www.weareteachers.com/restorative-justice/

Wilkerson, I. (2020). *Caste: The Lies That Divide Us* (p. 70). New York: Random House.

Woodson, J., & López, R. (2022). *The Year We Learned To Fly.* New York: Penguin Random House LLC.

World Fair Trade Organization. (2022, January 31). *History of fair trade.* https://wfto.com/about-us/history-wfto/history-fair-trade

Young, M.F.D. (1971). *Knowledge and Control. New Directions for the Sociology of Education.* London: Collier Macmillan.

Total Inclusivity and Us
Section II

Language and Microaggressions
Chapter Five

Throughout Section Two, we explore how our interactions with others contribute to, or impede, our journey to becoming more equitable and inclusive schools. In this opening chapter, we examine the political and power dimensions of language.

We may grow up learning the rhyme 'sticks and stones will break my bones, but words will never hurt me', but the message it conveys is, at best, misleading and, at worst, downright negligent. Words hurt. Think about an argument where you felt personally attacked or criticised. Maybe you were called selfish or lazy or assigned any number of other negative characteristics. Did you care? Did it heal quickly? Unless you are incredibly thick-skinned, the chances are that you ruminated on these words, felt angry about them, wanted to say hurtful words back and perhaps even believed them about yourself. Words have that effect – they stick around and hold immense power in either denying a person's identity (e.g. the 'deadnaming' of a trans person, i.e. referring to them by the name they no longer use) or undermining one's sense of self.

Language matters; it is the vehicle through which power structures and understandings of how the world works and people's place within it are shared, expressed, reproduced and changed. You cannot hold biases, beliefs or stereotypes without articulating them.

Language reflects not only our beliefs but also the culture we uphold. It is the primary means of signalling the cultural norms of a given workplace or school and can convey damaging ideas. Language has the potential to do harm irrespective of intent. However, language can also be a force for resistance and liberation from oppression and discrimination.

Think about the schools you have worked in and take a moment to reflect on what norms the language in those schools conveyed in terms of who was accepted and who was not. If you look closely,

67 Language and Microaggressions

DOI: 10.4324/9781003231233-7

language will always reveal what and who is really valued in an organisation.

We may like to think that people generally have become more sensitive when it comes to language, particularly given the rising influence of 'cancel culture'. Indeed, many people would like to believe that when it comes to the subject of racism, sexism, homophobia and ableism, they would be able to identify discriminatory behaviour.

However, what we think our beliefs are and how they actually play out in reality are not always one and the same.

To this end, as part of the discussion regarding language and how to communicate with others, it is important to understand the difference between respect and dignity and use this as our anchor point when it comes to guiding our communications. Whilst *respect* and *dignity* may often be used interchangeably, it is important to distinguish between the two. The word *respect* refers to the admiration one shows towards another person because of their abilities, achievements or status (how many times do we hear that 'respect is earned!'). Respect is conditional, and when you throw a power dynamic into the mix, such as employer/employee or teacher/student, things get a little complex. 'Dignity', on the other hand, should be unconditional, as it conveys the notion that everyone has inherent value and worth and should be treated accordingly (Kuhn, 2018).

As educators and leaders, we should all be aspiring to create cultures of dignity. One of the ways in which we can do this is through the norms that we create when it comes to our use of language and our communications with others.

As such, we felt that it was important to dedicate this chapter to highlight the subtle yet powerful ways in which 'othering' takes place (and is normalised) through one aspect of language that is pertinent to understand: microaggressions, or as more recently described by Jana (2020) ""subtle acts of exclusion" because there is nothing "micro" about them". As we explore in the following, if left unchallenged, such behaviour is not just problematic; it is also unsafe.

MICROAGGRESSIONS IN ACTION

Before delving deeper into definitions, let us ask you if you have come across any phrases like these in your schools, on your Facebook feeds, or in conversations with colleagues (and/or maybe you've even said them yourselves):

That's so gay.
All Lives Matter.
I'm not racist. I have friends who are Black.
The way that you have overcome your disability is so inspiring … you are so brave.
Wow, you speak such good English.

If you've ever heard or experienced any phrases like these (which is pretty much 100% likely), then you have heard microaggressions in action.

WHAT ARE MICROAGGRESSIONS?

The concept of microaggressions has become incorporated into the popular lexicon in recent years, as well as being widely studied in academic fields. Whilst initially defined in terms of covert forms of racial discrimination, they have since come to be more widely defined as the "brief and commonplace daily verbal, behavioral, and environmental indignities, whether intentional or unintentional, that communicate hostile, derogatory, or negative racial, gender, sexual orientation, and religious slights and insults to the target person or group" (Sue, 2010, p. 5). They are one such outgrowth of implicit bias and illustrate how biases manifest in our language (Finley, 2019). Although they are often unintentional and can be committed by people who view themselves as good and decent, they, in fact, have the effect of communicating a whole spectrum of negative hidden messages or 'metacommunications' betraying biased beliefs or attitudes (Sue, 2021).

Microaggressions tend to be targeted towards historically marginalised groups, including Black, Indigenous and People of Colour (BIPOC), LGBTQ+ persons, women and disabled people. The metacommunications that are present in these everyday slights and insults have several impacts:

- They invalidate an individual's identity and reality.
- They have a demeaning impact on an individual and their group identity.

- They communicate to an individual that they are in some way a lesser human being.
- They suggest to an individual that they do not belong to the dominant group.
- They relegate to an inferior status and treatment.

(Adapted from Sue, 2010)

Take a moment to pause and think back to a time when perhaps you have heard one of the phrases described earlier, or any time when you felt invalidated, particularly if it related to your own identity. How did it feel? Were you angry or upset? Did it cause confusion? Did you feel unsure about how to respond? Were you able to return to your day as normal after hearing an invalidating comment, or did it impact the tasks that you were doing? Did it cause you to doubt yourself?

What about if you haven't heard one of these phrases or if none of the earlier examples resonates with you? Here we'd encourage you to take a moment to reflect on whether you may have been the perpetrator of some of these microaggressive behaviours. We know that we, the authors, certainly have before truly learning and understanding the impact of them. Reflecting on this will help us to see the world, and the interactions we are a part of through a new lens – one that comes from the perspective of dignity.

We know that different groups and different intersecting identities experience microaggressions to differing degrees. You could think of a microaggression like a blister. It's uncomfortable and irritating, but you can deal with it. However, if you get blisters every day that continue to reopen and re-blister before they have a chance to heal, they can become overwhelming and even debilitating. Microaggressions, much like blisters, can have a cumulative effect, and after a while, the constant erasure of identity can cause lasting, long-term harm.

Microaggressions serve as constant reminders of being regarded as less than, and they have a hugely significant and detrimental effect over time. This has led to psychologists terming these everyday slights and insults (for historically marginalised groups in particular) as "death by a thousand cuts" (Sue, 2021).

Research has shown that being subject to microaggressions can lead to a whole range of psychological consequences, such as depression, anxiety, and trauma (see Nadal, 2018, for a detailed exploration of microaggressions and trauma). The stakes can be extremely high, and we as educators need to be aware that microaggressions take place amongst and between our students much earlier (and more often) than we might think. Previous research has shown that children become aware of race at a very early age. At 3 months of age, babies show a preference for faces belonging to certain ethnic groups, and at 9 months old, they can categorise faces based on race. Concerningly, by only 3 years of age, children can start to associate negative traits based on race (e.g. Black men are bad), and by age 4, they can start to associate white people with greater wealth and status (Sullivan, Wilton, and Apfelbaum, 2021).

One example which we'd like you to think about for a moment comes from one of our authors and highlights how microaggressive behaviours need not be outwardly sexist/racist/homophobic to have a negative and lasting impact. She explains:

> When I migrated to Australia I was in a school where there were only a handful of families of colour (mostly SE Asian background) in the community. The primary school I went to was a non-secular government school and we were given a picture of Santa to colour in to make Christmas cards with. I started to colour his hair black, because from my perspective people have black hair. I was immediately laughed at for doing this, and as a result this became a really negative experience for me.

The failure on our part as educators to acknowledge the 'stories' that we share as the norm (predominantly Western, white and heteronormative) may neglect the cultural influences and intersectional identities of our students. Now we'll unpack in more detail the different types of microaggressions and how they can manifest in our language and our behaviours.

WHAT ARE THE DIFFERENT TYPES OF MICROAGGRESSIONS?

According to Sue et al. (2007), microaggressions can take on three different forms: microassaults, microinsults and microinvalidations. Before looking at these in more detail, it is important to note that within the different types of microaggressions, there are also differences that exist in the 'metacommunications' that are communicated through them, and the subsequent impact that they have on different historically marginalised groups. Furthermore, how microaggressions manifest themselves will differ across contexts and according to the conventional stereotypes that are prevalent within that space. For example, as you'll come to read more about later, sexual objectification is a common type of microaggression experienced predominantly by women but rarely by men (irrespective of their racial group). Even within marginalised groups, microaggressions are not experienced in the same way. For example, it is highly like that white cisgender lesbians will have a very different experience of microaggressions than transgender individuals that are also BIPOC, even though they are both from the LGBTQ+ community. So let's explore these different forms of microaggressions in more detail (as described in Sue and Spanierman, 2020).

What Are Microassaults?

The first type of microaggressions is known as microassaults, and these are the easiest to identify. They are more explicit and outwardly discriminatory and resemble what we most likely think of when we think of racist or discriminatory behaviour. Sue (2010, p. 28) describes them as "conscious, deliberate and either subtle or explicit … biased attitudes, beliefs, or behaviors that are communicated to marginalized groups through environmental cues, verbalizations, or behaviors." In this respect, it is clear that microassaults have the sole intent to cause harm towards BIPOC, women, LGBTQ+ persons and disabled individuals.

What Are Microinsults?

The second type of microaggression is a microinsult. These are described as "communications that convey rudeness and insensitivity and demean a person's racial heritage or identity" (Sue, et al., 2007, p. 274). Microinsults not only tend to be unconscious but can also be both conscious and intentional. Sue and Spanierman (2020) outline six common themes of microinsults: ascription of intelligence, assumption of abnormality, criminality/assumption of criminal status, pathologizing cultural values/communication styles, second-class citizen and sexual objectification. Let's take a look at these in a bit more detail.

Ascription of Intelligence

This type of microinsult relates to the notion that levels of intelligence, competence, and abilities differ between racial groups. You might see the assumption that, for example, a student will be especially talented at maths or science because they are Asian.

We may also see ascriptions of intelligence related to gender when, for example, a teacher may act surprised when a female student excels at a 'traditionally masculine' subject such as computer science or engineering. This signals that having a female student who is talented in this subject is somewhat of a rarity. As a further example, how many times have we all heard both teachers and students alike say that a talented female athlete is "good for a girl"?

Assumption of Abnormality

This form of microinsult speaks to a person's race, gender or sexual orientation and implies that it is abnormal or deviant. An example of this would be when a student who is perceived to be 'odd' or nonconforming by other students, is called 'gay'. This type of microinsult is also present when members of the LGBTQ+ community are seen to be promiscuous or sexually deviant. Sadly, many of us can imagine that two boys holding hands would in many school contexts lead to stares and negative comments.

Criminality/Assumption of Criminal Status

This form of microinsult refers to the notion that a person is more likely to be criminal or dangerous due to their race. There are many examples of this, but one that made news headlines internationally involved a white woman who called the police about a Black man who was bird watching in Central Park in New York. During this incident, the woman called 911 and falsely accused the man of assaulting her after he had asked her to put her dog on its leash to prevent it from scaring away birds (BBC, 2020).

In a school environment, this type of microinsult could look like the setting of low expectations for students of colour in terms of behaviour or disciplining students of colour more harshly for minor issues because they are viewed as 'troublemakers' (for more information, see Gilliam et al., 2016).

Pathologising Cultural Values/Communication Styles

This particular form of microinsult refers to the idea that the cultural values and styles of communication of white heterosexual Western men are the norm and that by definition, the cultural values of marginalised groups are not the norm. This might be exemplified by a Western teacher asking an East Asian student to "speak up and ask more questions" because they feel that they are not engaging in the class. What the teacher has failed to understand is that there could be numerous reasons for this apparent lack of engagement. For example, the student may keep quiet due to the fear of losing face if they publicly make a mistake. Or, if the student is a second-language English speaker, a reluctance to express views may be impacted by their conceptual fluency when it comes to their language ability (Xia, 2009). A reaction to such behaviour (e.g. a teacher writing in the student's report that they are too quiet and don't contribute enough in class) indicates that students are expected to assimilate to the cultural values at play in their specific school environment. What is particularly problematic about this type of microinsult is that it can lead to the pathologising of certain groups and their identities – that they are abnormal by default.

Second-Class Citizen

This type of microinsult is remarkably common and conveys the unconscious message that certain groups are less worthy. Unless you belong to a historically marginalised group, you might even have trouble imagining it. It can happen in meetings at school when, for example, BIPOC or female teachers may be dismissed or talked over consistently and are therefore unable to share their views. It can occur when a young female teacher is mistaken for a student (which happened to one of the authors when going for an interview at a new school). You may think that such a simple mistake is not worthy of the label of 'microinsult', and yet what these types of incidents demonstrate is the overriding assumption that young females cannot possibly hold positions of authority. One of the other authors of this book had a very similar experience:

> When new to my school I once visited the Secondary staffroom, which was located in a different building on the same campus, to find another

member of staff. A teacher who did not know me approached and scolded me for being in a teacher-only space. I (a primary teacher) intentionally avoided that space for a very long time afterwards, and still recall that memory often whenever I step into that staffroom to this day!

The questions are, Who is this type of microinsult more likely to happen to? and What is the impact of this? Embarrassment and upset perhaps in the short term, but it can have a much deeper and damaging effect on one's sense of self in the longer term.

Sexual Objectification

Sexual objectification involves the dehumanising of women into 'objects' that are there for the sexual benefit of others (usually men). This dehumanisation also has a complex interaction with race and is illustrated in the exoticisation and sexualisation of Asian women. As much as we may not like to admit it, this behaviour undoubtedly takes place not only in our classrooms but also in our staffrooms. As one female teacher once commented to our authors, she stopped going into her school staffroom at lunchtimes because she often found that many of the male staff would either talk openly about their sexual relationships or would suddenly become silent when women entered the staffroom. When schools create or enable cultures where this objectification is normalised and unchallenged, this has dire consequences. The endemic problems currently faced by schools relating to the sharing of 'nudes' illustrates this point. Another teacher shared with us how poorly she felt that an incident was handled at her previous school, during which a female student disclosed that she was being pressured by an older man online to continually send more and more inappropriate photos of herself under the threat of them being made public if she did not comply. The first response of the administration was to focus on the actions of the student: "But why did you send them to him in the first place?" In this case, the young, vulnerable, female student was blamed for her own sexual objectification rather than criticism being directed at the online predator who had targeted her.

There are many other examples of how sexual objectification is (knowingly or unknowingly) encouraged in our schools, and some pertinent examples include the following:

- School uniforms and dress codes – particularly for female students
- The language teachers use, especially in early childhood, which normalizes the objectification of girls, for example 'You look so pretty!'
- Rape culture and language that is openly disrespectful of women
- Educating girls about the risks of unprotected sex, date rape, sexual assault and so on rather than focusing on teaching boys about their responsibilities for understanding consent

This is why it is so important to examine the difference between intent and impact – for example what is the intent behind the gendering of school uniforms, and what might be the impact on how children see themselves? Is it truly necessary to make female students wear skirts if they don't feel comfortable doing so?

WHAT ARE MICROINVALIDATIONS?

The third type of microaggressions is known as microinvalidations and can be defined as "communications that exclude, negate, or nullify the psychological thoughts, feelings, or experiential reality of a Person of Color" (Sue et al., 2007, p. 274). Microinvalidations can be both verbal and nonverbal and, as argued by Sue and Spanierman (2020), in many ways actually represent the most damaging form of microaggression, as they gradually and subtly work to deny an individual's racial, gender or sexual-orientation reality. Sue and Spanierman (2020) put forward four main microinvalidation themes: alien in one's own land, colour, gender and sexual-orientation blindness, denial of individual racism/sexism/heterosexism and the myth of meritocracy.

Alien in One's Own Land

This type of microinvalidation relates to an individual being continually perceived as a foreigner in their own country. Comments like "Where are you from?" and "You speak really good English!" make the assumption that a person of colour is foreign-born and, depending on the national context in which it is said, has the underlying message of 'you are not [insert relevant nationality]'.

Colour, Gender and Sexual-Orientation Blindness

This type of microinvalidation is often conveyed through an unwillingness to see or acknowledge someone's true identity in terms of their colour, gender and sexual orientation and, as a result, fails to recognise the oppression experienced by these groups and intersecting identities. Comments such as "When I see you, I don't see colour" and "We are all one human race" or the infamous "All Lives Matter" are common microinvalidations towards people of colour that you might hear in conversations or on social media feeds. Comments such as these indicate that the person saying it, on one hand, does not want to acknowledge race (and doesn't allow for race to be brought into a discussion) and, on the other, is dismissing the fact that race can be integral to understanding a person's lived experience. Whilst some comments that demonstrate a "blindness" towards these aspects of our identities may seem to be done as a way to not appear racist/sexist/homophobic, Sue et al. (2007) argue that denying these factors actually serves to deny identity.

Everyone's experience is not the same (e.g. not all families consist of a mother and a father, rather families come in many different forms!) We must remember this in our schools and remain open and curious to this fact.

Denial of Individual Racism/Sexism/Genderism/Heterosexism

This type of microaggression is used as a way of subverting or denying one's own personal bias (much like "colour, gender and sexual-orientation blindness") and rejects the notion that an individual is capable of bias, whether that be racism, sexism or homophobia. As we know, it's often those that present as 'decent' people that can also hold views and communicate in ways that demonstrate their biases. This includes comments such as "I'm not racist. I have Black friends" or "As a leader (or teacher), I always treat males and females the same." Having non-white friends doesn't excuse someone from holding racial biases, as chances are you unconsciously take on board messages that view non-white people as less than. A school principal can claim to treat male and female staff the same whilst participating in the 'boys club' of school directors, socialising with and mentoring male staff and predominantly promoting male staff to leadership roles. Assertions are not actions, and they don't magically protect you from developing, and acting on, biases.

Myth of Meritocracy

This type of microaggression states that race, gender, sexuality, class, disability, age, religion and language do not have any bearing on life successes at all and is closely related to the "colour, gender and sexual-orientation blindness" microinvalidation. It assumes that we all, regardless of our social identities and lived experiences, have the same chance to succeed, if only we work hard enough. Within this myth, there is no acknowledgement that the systemic forces at play disproportionality affect historically marginalised groups in terms of poverty, access to education (and particularly elite forms of education) and educational attainment. This is where it is important to acknowledge the difference between equity and equality. Equality ensures that we treat students and staff the same, whereas equity means that we acknowledge that students and staff are given support and resources based on their individual needs. Are our schools focusing on treating people the same or attending to our differences?

DISABILITY AND ABLEIST MICROAGGRESSIONS

A school that is totally inclusive must be aware of the challenges of disabled people; those whose disabilities are both visible and invisible. Much of the discussions taking place around microaggressions have tended to be heavily centred on racial and LGBTQ+ identities and experiences, and much less is known or discussed when it comes to disabled people and their experiences of disability-specific microaggressions – or on the impact of the intersections of disability with other historically marginalised identities.

Ableist microaggressions refer to brief or covert insults or slights that are aimed towards individuals based on their disability, and centre non-disabled experiences of the world as the norm (Keller and

Galgay, 2010). Researchers Richard Keller and Corinne Galgay sought to uncover the patterns of microaggressions that were experienced by individuals based on their disability and in doing so identified eight main themes of ableist microaggression: denial of personal identity ("I can't believe that you are married" – people see the disability first and are surprised to learn about other aspects of a disabled person's life), denial of disability experience ("we all have some form of disability" – a disabled person's experiences are minimised and seen as not as important), denial of privacy ("what happened to you" – not allowing an individual privacy regarding their disability), helplessness (when people try to help disabled people without asking because they assume they cannot do anything because a person is disabled), secondary gain ("we are raising money to help the local special needs school" – people expect to feel good for helping individuals with disabilities), spread effect ("deaf people can't speak properly" – when expectations about an individual are based on one specific disability), infantilization "let me do that for you" – you are not capable of doing this and need my help), patronisation ("you are so inspiring" – you are special for living as a disabled person), second-class citizen (that school only makes accessibility changes when it has a disabled student, or when a student complains that a facility is not accessible, they are seen as bothersome) and desexualisation ("I would never be in a relationship with a wheelchair user", "I could never date an autistic person" – a disabled person is denied their sexuality and/or cannot be viewed as attractive).

CONCLUSION

A knowledge of microaggressions is essential for educators and leaders in order to help us all better understand the negative experiences of many marginalised people, groups and intersecting identities. This includes our staff, our students and our friends and families. A better understanding of microaggressions and "making the 'invisible', visible" (Sue and Spanierman, 2020, p. 29) is the first step towards challenging and dismantling unconscious racism, sexism, homophobia and ableism, because it allows us to create space to put words to something that is often difficult to describe. It also allows us to talk about the impact of this in our schools, and on our students and staff (Sue and Spanierman, 2020). There are those who may attempt to dismiss the impact of microaggressions as 'harmless' or 'unintentional', but the presence of microaggressions often signals that we are enabling inequitable and discriminatory social norms. When we take steps to confront and eliminate the use of microaggressions, we also open the door to wider conversations about examining and challenging bias and ensuring the dignity of all.

You may not remember all the different types of microaggressions, but what we do hope you will come away with is a greater awareness of when they arise in our own interactions and a greater understanding of the harm that our words cause. Rather than focusing on the labelling and categorising of behaviours, what we must focus on is whether we are a part of normalising harmful language in our schools or not. We need to reflect on whether we are taking action and being an upstander or being a bystander and letting things go unchallenged.

CHAPTER FIVE: REFLECTIONS, GUIDANCE AND COMMITMENTS

Reflection Exercise: Whilst reading this chapter we hope you will have been prompted to reflect on when you may have used language that was experienced by another as a microaggression. Reflect further on this. Was it a result of your implicit bias? Did your intent match the impact? What happened after this offence was made?

Have you been the recipient of such microaggressions and how did that make you feel? When did those moments occur in your personal life or in your professional life as an educator? In what context did the microaggressions arise – were they framed around sexuality, gender, age, religion, ethnicity, nationality or an intersection of multiple identity factors? It is important to recognise that we can be both perpetrators and victims. When were you one or both?

Guidance: As educators we have a clear responsibility to ensure our students are protected from any and all forms of abuse. This book offers guidance, but you can delve much further into this by reading and exploring how language can be weaponised in education. Become knowledgeable and pass that knowledge on to others. Interrupt microaggressions by calling them out and where appropriate calling people in to unpack together why it was problematic. In doing so you'll acquire a deeper understanding and critical awareness of the impact of language and microaggressions in action.

Commitment: The most important commitment you can make is to be prepared to challenge abusive language and microaggressions, especially in your school. Don't accept microaggressions from either students or staff simply because it has become normalised in a school's culture. Don't be a bystander, be an upstander instead.

REFERENCES

BBC. (2020). Central Park: Amy Cooper 'made second racist call' against birdwatcher. BBC. www.bbc.com/news/world-us-canada-54544443.

Finley, T. (2019). A Look at Implicit Bias and Microaggressions. Edutopia. www.edutopia.org/article/look-implicit-bias-and-microaggressions.

Gilliam, W. S., Maupin, A. N., Reyes, C. R., Accavitti, M., & Shic, F. (2016). Do Early Educators' Implicit Biases Regarding Sex and Race Relate to Behavior Expectations and Recommendations of Preschool Expulsions and Suspensions? Yale Child Study Center. www.medicine.yale.edu/childstudy/zigler/publications/Preschool%20Implicit%20Bias%20Policy%20Brief_final_9_26_276766_5379_v1.pdf.

Jana, T. (2020). Initiating the Important Conversations around Microaggressions. CEOWORLD Magazine. https://ceoworld.biz/2020/03/05/initiating-the-important-conversations-around-microaggressions/

Keller, R. M., & Galgay, C. E. (2010). Microaggressive experiences of people with disabilities. In D. W. Sue (eds.) Microaggressions and Marginality: Manifestation, Dynamics, and Impact (pp. 241–267). New Jersey: John Wiley & Sons.

Kuhn, C. (2018). What's The Difference Between Dignity and Respect? Cultures of Dignity. www.culturesofdignity.com/difference-between-dignity-and-respect/.

Nadal, K. L. (2018). Microaggressions and Traumatic Stress: Theory, Research, and Clinical Treatment. Washington, DC: American Psychological Association.

Sue, D. W. (2010). Microaggressions in Everyday Life: Race, Gender, and Sexual Orientation. Hoboken, NJ: John Wiley & Sons.

Sue, D. W. (2021). Microaggressions: Death by a Thousand Cuts. Scientific American. www.scientificamerican.com/article/microaggressions-death-by-a-thousand-cuts/.

Sue, D. W., Capodilupo, C. M., Torino, G. C., Bucceri, J. M., Holder, A. M. B., Nadal, K. L., & Esquilin, M. (2007). Racial microaggressions in everyday life: Implications for clinical practice, American Psychologist, 62(4): 271–286.

Sue, D. W., & Spanierman, L. B. (2020). Microaggressions in everyday life (2nd ed.). Hoboken, NJ: John Wiley & Sons.

Sullivan, J., Wilton, L., & Apfelbaum, E. P. (2021). Adults Delay Conversations About Race Because They Underestimate Children's Processing of Race, *Journal of Experimental Psychology: General*, 150(2): 395–400.

Xia, S. (2009). Are They Ready to Participate? East Asian Students' Acquisition of Verbal Participation in American Classrooms. *Issues in Applied Linguistics*, 17(2): 137–157.

Chapter Six

Schools play an undeniably important role in the safeguarding of children and young people. We all know that safeguarding is not simply best practice but a vital mechanism that should be at the heart of education. Schools must be safe places.

Safeguarding, in its modern form, can be traced back to the 1970s. In the UK, the 1973 murder of 7-year-old Maria Colwell by her stepfather, shortly after she returned from foster care, highlighted the devastating failings of the child protection system at the time. As such, the need to revise this system to ensure that professionals were able to recognise and respond to concerns of abuse and/or neglect, led to the introduction of the Children Act 1975 (NSPCC, 2021). Since then, there have been a number of essential developments both in the UK and internationally, including the 1990 United Nations Convention on the Rights of the Child. In the UK, the establishment of a centralised criminal records check system and reforms to the way in which people are vetted before working with children followed the tragic killing of Holly Wells and Jessica Chapman, both aged 10, by their school caretaker. International schools and accrediting agencies similarly tightened up their processes and the International Taskforce on Child Protection was founded, following an FBI investigation into allegations of widespread sexual abuse committed by a former international school teacher.

As educators and leaders reading this book, you'll be all too aware of the role that schools play when it comes to safeguarding and the ongoing commitment required to ensuring that we have the necessary systems in place to keep children safe. We'd encourage you to just pause for a moment here, and ask yourself a few questions about the schools in which you work:

DOI: 10.4324/9781003231233-8

1. Does your school have a child protection policy?
2. Does your school have a policy that safeguards both students and staff?
3. Does your school have a policy that addresses diversity, equity and inclusion?

Whilst your answer to question 1 will be a resounding yes, perhaps it's a maybe to numbers 2 and/or 3? Of course, you hope that staff are protected as much as students, but perhaps you're not 100% sure? You know there have been ongoing discussions regarding diversity, equity and inclusion, but you need to double-check what's actually in place?

We now encourage you to take a moment to think about how these three questions interrelate because taken together they signal how far a school is towards Total Inclusivity, the nurturing, valuing and protection of all identities.

We know that safeguarding in schools should consist of child protection policies, clear and sensitive channels of communication and support from outside agencies. However, it is important to move beyond thinking about safeguarding as merely the prevention of harm and encompass thinking about how we create equitable environments that are safe for all.

This is why a focus on Total Inclusivity is so important. If we are not tackling implicit bias, if we are not putting robust diversity, equity and inclusion policies in place, and if we are not ensuring that everyone in our school community is safe to be their authentic selves, then we are not safeguarding for all.

WHAT IS A SAFE SCHOOL THAT SAFEGUARDS ALL?

We posit that a safe school consists of four layers (as shown in Figure 6.1, model adapted from Bronfenbrenner's 1979 ecological systems theory). These are children and young people, faculty and support staff, leadership and support structures and an overarching culture of care. It is important to note that these are not distinct concentric layers but, rather, layers that can shift and press upon one another, that can open and give space to one another. We'll go into more depth about each of these in turn, starting with the core of a safe school – the children and young people we are there to guide and support.

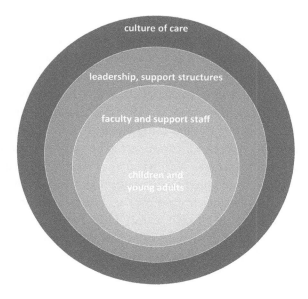

Figure 6.1 Layers of a Safe School

CHILDREN AND YOUNG PEOPLE

At the innermost core of a safe school are the children and young adults we work with. These are the young people that come to us with unique life experiences and identities, differing support structures and family ecosystems. If we take a moment to think about the students in our schools and their intersecting identities, do we know how they feel in our schools? Most important, do we know if they feel safe?

One of the writers of this book was recently speaking with senior students about creating curriculum vitae (CVs) for undertaking work experience. There was a discussion about what information should be included on a CV and whether photos should be included. One of the students, surveying her work, remarked, "I hate this photo, it makes me look so Asian". When asked to explore this sentiment further, they explained that there are a lot of stereotypes about Thai women and that in the past, when some people had found out that they were both Thai and European, they would be subjected to jokes about whether they had a penis, due to the stereotype that Thai women are 'Kathoeys' (otherwise known as 'ladyboys'). The same student also commented that they were concerned about leaving home to attend

university, due to the increase in Asian hate crimes in the UK and US. The student explained that because they were 'white passing', they didn't really want people to know that they were Asian, because they were worried about how they would be treated. They also said that whilst they felt confident to challenge these discriminatory comments when they occurred, they were worried that not all of their friends were. However, what was interesting about this discussion was that the students didn't deem such comments to be racist behaviour due to the frequency and casualness with which they were so often delivered.

Whilst it's not clear whether this behaviour occurred within the school context or outside, it does give us insight into how students view themselves and the discriminatory behaviours that they experience on a regular basis. It demonstrates how racist comments such as these can become normalised when they happen regularly. And how, for those on the receiving end of such behaviour, it can become 'easier' or more advantageous to hide parts of your identity, for example to come across as 'less Asian', avoid unwanted comments, or reduce the risk of being viewed less favourably by prospective employers.

That such experiences are being shared directly by students certainly makes us question whether they feel safe to be who they are. Schools are one of the key socialising agents for children and young people, and as such, it is important that steps are taken to empower them to be their authentic selves. This is discussed later in this chapter.

FACULTY AND SUPPORT STAFF

Moving outwards in Figure 6.1, young people are surrounded by members of faculty and support staff who are there to teach, empower and guide the students that they work with. That's us! Like our students, we also bring our unique selves to our work; our education histories and life stories, our beliefs and values and all the other parts of us that make us who we are. Faculty and support staff play an important role in the identification of harm and taking the necessary steps to pass on safeguarding concerns to a Designated Safeguarding Lead. Staff are very often the adults young people learn from and model. The behaviours exhibited by adults send messages to young people about what is acceptable behaviour and what is the norm. This also goes for what adults choose to address and what they leave out or ignore – in this regard, inaction is also a teacher. This is the hidden curriculum;

"the unwritten, unofficial, and often unintended lessons, values, and perspectives that students learn in school" (Great Schools Partnership, 2015).

Students learn from us how to be in the world, and how to interact with others. They learn about who is awarded higher 'status' in different contexts, and how power dynamics work. One of the authors commented on how students seem to sense the vulnerability of new staff and how they will often try to push the boundaries with them because they can sense a lack of confidence and experience. She felt that as a young female member of staff, she initially had a harder time establishing boundaries with students than some of her male colleagues who started teaching at the same time. From her perspective, it appeared that the male staff often seemed to demand more respect from students, more quickly.

Was it that they were bigger in stature and had a greater physical presence? Was it that they were better and just knew how to manage the classroom more effectively? Or was it that students viewed male teachers differently than female teachers and adjusted their behaviour accordingly? Truth is, it's hard to say, and it may be a combination of these different factors. Regardless, it is important to reflect on not only how students view and interact with teachers but also how teachers interact with each other. As we've all experienced, students are incredibly perceptive and can pick up on the relationships that we have with our colleagues. Therefore, we must consider, for example, how white teachers interact with teachers who are Black, Indigenous and People of Colour, how LGBTQ+ or gender-non-conforming teachers are spoken to or about, how female teachers are viewed and the roles they hold and how managers and senior leaders treat the staff under their care.

One teacher working at an international school in South-East Asia mentioned to us that they had observed that the local staff in their school tended to be teaching assistants, housekeeping or maintenance staff. They also felt that the local teaching staff were seen to be 'lower' on the school hierarchy by its predominantly white, Western management team. This teacher commented:

These staff are really good at their jobs, and when you talk with them you find out they have Masters degrees, and so much experience, so it's difficult to hear that they are paid much less than the foreign teachers. Students pick up on this difference too, and they definitely don't behave as well for the local teachers. You can also see that there isn't much interaction between the local and international teachers. They never really get the chance to air their concerns or ideas at staff meetings, and are almost positioned as separate within the school. It really concerns me to think about how this must make the local staff feel - and the message this will be sending to our students.

Another way in which children and young people and faculty and support staff overlap and have a symbiotic relationship can be seen in the movement to better recognise and respect the diversity of gender identities. One step towards doing that is the inclusion of gender pronouns. Some schools have really embraced the inclusion of pronouns, whether in email signatures or on a wider basis, for example asking students to share their pronouns when meeting a new class for the first time. They recognise that this seemingly small gesture is actually very powerful and allows students (and staff) to take ownership of their identity. Other schools have expressed a hesitancy to do this. In order to still appear inclusive, they may state that it is up to the individual teacher if they want to do so, but that they will not be making it a mandatory change. Some have banned the practice entirely. As one teacher told us:

I went to my Principal and asked about the inclusion of pronouns in our email signatures and they couldn't understand why it was important. I felt that it was a way to signal to our students that we are open and receptive of all gender identities, and let them know that we are people that they can come to if they have questions about exploring their gender and sexuality. As a member of the LGBTQ+ community myself, I was really saddened by the response I got.

The dismissal of this teacher's request was not simply a disagreement with an idea — it was also a dismissal of their identity. It was not only the lack of knowledge that upset the teacher but the refusal to learn why this request was important to both them and their students.

The use of pronouns can be one way to signal the acceptance of diverse gender identities within a school and foster a culture of acceptance. Note, however, that to move beyond tokenism, such actions must be followed up with structural changes and policies that tackle LGBTQ+ inclusion in a meaningful way.

LEADERSHIP AND SUPPORT STRUCTURES

Moving outwards again, surrounding and encompassing the students and staff, are the leadership and support structures within a school. As we will all know from working in schools, whilst the structures and layers of leadership may appear relatively similar from school to school, the quality of these structures can certainly vary. Good safeguarding practice, in the traditional sense, requires there to be a point of contact for coordinating interventions when it comes to children who are safeguarding concerns. These may not necessarily be members of the leadership team, because of the conflict of interest that can arise from also wanting to protect the school. This conflict can also manifest in the resistance we may observe from leaders when asked to create more diverse and equitable environments.

When it comes to the expectations of behaviour and ethics of leadership, these are fully within the school's remit to shape and influence. What is deemed acceptable behaviour by staff (and leadership) is partly written in the school's code of conduct. However, in order to truly ensure that these standards are upheld, the cultural norms of a school (i.e. the unwritten rules passed on by behaviors and interactions in the school community) must be consistent with this. There is no use in saying that it is within a school's mission to promote diversity and inclusion, when there is a lack of diversity on executive boards and in leadership teams. When it comes to leadership and creating more equitable schools, we must move beyond a sole focus on representation, and reflect on whether there is diversity in the voices being heard. Similarly, what can be seen in much of the vital diversity, equity and inclusion work taking place is that these often are grassroots movements instigated by teachers, many of whom have marginalised identities. Much of this important work is unpaid and places a huge amount of pressure on teachers who may already feel vulnerable when it comes to their position within a school. Take for example the queer educator mentioned earlier, who was advocating for the simple change to include pronouns in staff email signatures. This teacher had to ask permission to share their identity from a cisgender, heterosexual male school leader who had never had to consider why this might be important. Sadly, such incidents are commonplace, and there are many educators who have had to fight to be open and honest about who they are within their schools and classrooms.

CULTURE OF CARE

A Totally Inclusive School must be situated in a culture of care, that is one that sees, values, protects and *celebrates* everyone for who they are.

It is important to note that a true culture of care can only exist if it comes from a genuine place of empathy and understanding. Being a Totally Inclusive School is not about paying lip service to change, and the work to develop our schools has to be done for the right reasons and in a way that ensures that everyone is heard. As such, a culture of care asks us at all levels of the school to be self-reflective and understand the motivations underpinning the work being done. This is where it is important to reflect on the intent versus the impact of what we do.

Take this example where a liberal, state-sponsored private school in Germany hosted a #BlackLivesMatter panel discussion titled Creating Safe Spaces. This student-led and head of school–endorsed event aimed to give both students, teachers and members of a local anti-racism activism group an opportunity to discuss matters related to racism. Although well intended, this one-off event involved the historically marginalised members of the school and local community being put on stage to speak in front of a camera about past trauma for the benefit of a predominantly white audience. Such events cause more harm to the historically marginalised instead of addressing it. It was equally unclear what the school's commitment and stance were on becoming an anti-discriminatory institution as there was no whole-school plan in place related to diversity, equality, inclusion and justice.

Now that we've had a chance to reflect on the intertwining and reciprocal layers of what makes a safe and secure environment for all, a piece of the puzzle that has been touched on here, but is often missing from conversations around safeguarding, is the safeguarding of staff. In the following, we discuss the five key forms of harm: (1) bullying, (2) neglect, (3) harassment, (4) discrimination and

(5) abuse (XR Training, 2012). The aim of this part of the chapter is to not replicate the explanations of these different forms of harm but to highlight some of the ways in which staff, particularly those with historically marginalised identities, can experience harm.

When it comes to the behaviours that cause harm to staff, schools have a tendency to ignore the 'red flags' that we might have recognised had the behaviour been directed at a child. It can be common for such behaviours to become normalised, dismissed or brushed over; such is the nature of school environments where many staff are often under a great deal of pressure to produce results. Damaging behaviour is easily excused if the 'ends justify the means'. Make no mistake though, these forms of harm are incredibly damaging, and must be addressed if and when they are identified. The safeguarding of staff against staff-on-staff harm, parent–staff harm or student–staff harm is just as important as child protection.

FORMS OF HARM

Forms of harm are behaviours that violate an individual's right to feel safe and secure. For the purposes of this book, we have outlined our own key distinctions and types of harm, which overlap with many other definitions of harm. However, the key behaviours that constitute these different forms of harm remain the same. To this end, the classification of behaviours is not of significance, but what is important is being able to give language to name forms of harm. If we can't name it, we can't address it.

Bullying

Bullying is considered to be a pattern of targeted, persistent behaviour that is

- Offensive, malicious or intimidating
- An abuse of power
- Intended to humiliate, undermine or injure an individual

(ACAS, 2021)

Bullying can take place via a variety of different mediums, including verbal, physical, or in online interactions. The bullying of staff can manifest in a range of different ways in a school, and this may include how an individual's work performance is evaluated and monitored (Healthline, 2019). Bullying can also be retaliatory in nature, such as the following example that was shared by a teacher:

> I was reported by my Head of Department to the Headteacher after my moderation of coursework was raised as a concern by an exam board. This was my first year collecting and evaluating evidence, and I had gone to my Head of Department on a number of occasions for support because I wanted to make sure that I was doing it correctly. I believed that I was advised poorly by my Head of Department, so when the exam board raised concerns, I disclosed this to the Headteacher. After this, my relationship with my Head of Department was never the same. Termly teaching evaluations became a personal attack, and I was constantly belittled in department meetings when trying to share my ideas. I was a young, female LGBTQ+ member of staff in an all-white, cis-male department. When I confided in another member of staff (a young, male teacher) he was sympathetic, but told me not to make a bigger issue out of it than it already was. He thought he was being supportive, but it was clear he just wasn't willing to stand up for me, for fear of jeopardizing his own position.

Harassment

Harassment can be defined as "unwanted behaviour which you find offensive or which makes you feel intimidated or humiliated" (Citizens Advice, 2022a). Harassment can occur on its own or may accompany other forms of discrimination. 'Unwanted behaviour' may include the following:

- spoken or written words or abuse
- offensive emails, tweets or comments on social networking sites
- images and graffiti
- physical gestures
- facial expressions
- jokes

(Citizens Advice, 2022a)

Discrimination

Discrimination can come in many different forms but refers to when someone is "treated differently and worse than someone else for certain reasons" (Citizens Advice, 2022b) based on their gender, sexuality, race, ethnicity, religion, age, disability and intersecting identities. This includes marginalised groups getting paid less or being hired in predominantly lower-paying positions, pay gaps between male and female staff of equal experience and/or qualifications, unfair discipline, unjustified rejection for jobs or promotions, being denied opportunities and being held to inconsistent standards (Equal Rights Advocates, 2019).

Abuse

Abuse can be physical, sexual and/or emotional in nature. In a workplace, abuse of a sexual nature can include someone repeatedly complimenting a member of staff on how they look, repeated unwanted touching, discussing someone's sex life or making sexual jokes, sending sexually suggestive messages or spreading sexual rumours and circulating nude images (Barreiro, n.d.).

Neglect

Neglect in a staff context refers to a school's inability to meet the basic needs of a member of staff. This may include issues such as poor workspace provision, a failure to minimise safety risks and/or preventable accidents, problems with data protection, a lack of (or poor) orientation or transition process, a lack of access to necessary professional development provision and delayed employment contract renewal (Verge Safety Barriers, 2018).

WHAT CONTRIBUTES TO A LACK OF SAFETY IN A SCHOOL?

An understanding of harm will help us in our journey to become a Totally Inclusive School. Each 'layer' of the safe school model is equally as important as the next – we cannot claim to have successfully created a culture of care if even one person within our community (student, staff or leader) feels unsafe.

An important question to ask ourselves is, 'What contributes to someone feeling unsafe?' Before moving on to read this part, perhaps take a moment to list some of the things that have affected your sense of safety whilst working in a school environment. Likewise, when you have felt safe and secure in a school environment, what have been the factors that have contributed to this?

Whilst this won't be an exhaustive list of all the factors that contribute to a sense of safety in schools (for staff), we assert that there are three fundamental considerations that when not attended to, contribute to a lack of safety in a workplace. These are (1) power dynamics, (2) vulnerable positions and (3) advocacy, alliances, and accountability.

POWER DYNAMICS

Many school structures are built on hierarchies of leadership, consisting of school boards, executive leadership teams, middle leaders, teachers, assistants, and other support staff and specialists. There will undoubtedly be positions that hold more decision-making power than others, but as many people may have experienced, power and influence may not always be directly tied to a particular position; it can also be tied to privileged markers of identity (white, male, heterosexual, cisgender). It might be interesting to take a moment to ask yourself how these look in your workplace. When we see our environments through a Total Inclusivity lens, things can start to appear a little different, and they are not always what they appear to be. This may be especially apparent when the person in the position of power is the one acting inappropriately. Take for example this excerpt from a colleague based in an international school:

> We had a staff anti-bullying policy at our school, and the person we had to report any concerns to was the school Principal. However, it was this same person that I witnessed treating several members of staff unfairly. They appeared to play favourites with some teachers, whilst other staff were treated poorly. Staff that challenged decisions were often shut down in meetings, or publicly criticised. The Principal would deliberately ignore emails, and give deadlines at short notice to people that they didn't like. When someone complained about this to the executive board, they were told that a discussion would be had with this person. Ultimately, no further action was taken, and the Principal in question continued to behave in the same manner.

This is an important example of power dynamics at play in several ways. First, the behaviour has had a harmful effect on those who are not 'favourites' (i.e. do not hold any power) in this organisation, for whatever reason that may be. Second, what's powerful about this example is what the lack of action on behalf of the executive team signals to other staff in the school, especially those who may have also been unfairly treated by this principal (or someone else in a position of power). It indicates to them what might happen if they challenge a decision or report inappropriate behaviour – nothing.

VULNERABLE POSITIONS

Have you ever witnessed something that you disagreed with as a staff member? If so, did you challenge it? What was the outcome of that challenge? If you didn't challenge something, what were the factors that led you to hold back?

As adults with bills to pay, and perhaps other people counting on us for support, we are economically vulnerable as school employees. How we seek to challenge or ask questions may differ from person to person, and whether we choose to air concerns is often influenced by how professionally vulnerable we feel we are. As we know from the earlier chapters, marginalised identities do experience implicit bias and discrimination, and therefore may be more vulnerable when challenging the status quo. An LGBTQ+ teacher shared with us that they and several of their colleagues had received an email from a senior member of staff in which a derogatory slang term was used as a joke. They were upset, and when they discussed it with other teachers, it was widely agreed that it had been unacceptable. And yet, no other staff members (even those who might have been considered less 'vulnerable' in terms of their position of power) were willing to publicly challenge or call out the use of language.

Developing an understanding of vulnerable positions will undoubtedly impact our approach to Total Inclusivity. If this is not something you had considered before, now that you have developed a greater awareness of 'professional vulnerability' and its impact on yourself and your colleagues, what, if anything, will you change? How will you do better? As we mentioned earlier in the chapter, our lack of action or silence can communicate just as much about our true intentions as our actions. Continue to reflect on this as you move through this book.

THE ROLE OF ADVOCACY, ALLIANCES AND ACCOUNTABILITY IN SAFEGUARDING

> Leaders don't claim to be victims of injustice. These take responsibility for stopping injustice. Leaders don't attack the powerless. They shield the powerless from attacks. Leaders don't assert greatness. They nurture greatness in others.
>
> (Grant, 2019)

As we have reflected in different ways in this book so far, schools are both a mirror of society and a catalyst for change. As educators and leaders reading this book, it is important that we understand and analyse how power dynamics function in a wider culture and where and how our schools sit within this. There is liberty within schools to mould and change them. Just as teachers are responsible for the culture of care they create in their classrooms, school leaders are responsible for the culture of care they create within their schools. There may be many challenges and hurdles, but change is and will always be possible.

Safeguarding for all must incorporate policies and protections for staff and students that place diversity, equity and inclusion at their core. Examples of policies that address safeguarding include those presented in Table 6.1.

Change can happen fast or slow or can be both at the same time. Three areas that can help facilitate or support change are advocacy, alliances and accountability.

We must advocate for change, and we must always reflect on a very important question: **What power do you have to support others?**

We must form alliances amongst all members of a school community to bring about positive change. We must use our power to support those who may be in more vulnerable positions than us, and we must use our voice for the collective good.

This includes having difficult and courageous conversations and holding ourselves and others accountable when our actions and cultural norms contradict being a Totally Inclusive institution. This is not the responsibility of marginalised individuals or groups; it is the responsibility that every single one of us must embrace.

Table 6.1 Example safeguarding policies

Adults	Overarching Policies	Students
• Anti-harassment policy • Safer recruitment processes • Board/Visitors/ Volunteer Handbook • Code of Conduct (Faculty) • Managing concerns and allegations process	• Safeguarding & Child Protection policy • Diversity, equity and inclusion policy • COVID-19 • Digital safety & protection policy • Mental health & Well-being policy • Whistleblowing & complaints process	• Behaviour & disciplinary policies • Peer-on-peer abuse policy • Trips/travel policy • Risk-management policy • Curriculum design

Based on the work of Katie Rigg, Director of Safeguarding and Student Well-being, Council of International Schools.

We can create safe spaces by increasing visibility and celebrating marginalised identities through the books we read, and the histories that we study. We can create them by signalling to others that they are welcome through small but meaningful acts, such as including pronouns on our email signatures. We can create them by building alliances and using our individual power to support others.

Most important, we must reflect, we must challenge, we must learn and we must change.

CHAPTER SIX: REFLECTIONS, GUIDANCE AND COMMITMENT

Reflections: How safe is your school (and not just in terms of security guards, background checks on new staff, or the Health and Safety policies)? How do you assess this? Are all the identities in your school protected, safeguarded and nurtured? To find out, you will have to do some research. Do your colleagues understand what it means for everyone in the school community to be safeguarded, and if not, what will you do to ensure they do?

Guidance: Creating safe spaces means creating a culture where people can be authentic. If you know that to be authentic means you wouldn't be accepted on account of your religion, sexuality, gender, nationality, ethnicity or race, then the institution's culture is not safe. And if it isn't safe for you, it isn't safe for anyone else.

Start this journey by creating safe spaces (if and when you can) — where staff and students can share their feelings and insecurities and be open about what they need to feel safe. Ask the leaders of the school to support this. Ideally, they will initiate it. If not, gather like-minded staff together and present this suggestion at a future meeting. Start the conversation; initiate the process.

Commitment: Don't be prepared to only accept conventional, traditional understandings of student safety. Recognise that student (and staff) safety must extend into the realms of the existential, the emotional, the felt. The school has a responsibility for creating an infrastructure that promotes safety so that all in the community feel a sense of belonging. Remember that the onus of 'belonging' is not on the marginalised but on the school.

REFERENCES

ACAS. (2021). Handling a bullying, harassment or discrimination complaint at work. *ACAS*. www.acas.org.uk/handling-a-bullying-harassment-discrimination-complaint.

Barreiro, S. (n.d.). What Kinds of Behaviors Are Considered Sexual Harassment? *NOLO*. https://www.nolo.com/legal-encyclopedia/what-kinds-of-behaviors-are-considered-sexual-harassment.html.

Bronfenbrenner, U. (1979). *The Ecology of Human Development: Experiments in Nature and Design*. Cambridge, MA: Harvard University Press.

Citizens Advice. (2022a). Harassment. *Citizens Advice*. https://www.citizensadvice.org.uk/law-and-courts/discrimination/what-are-the-different-types-of-discrimination/harassment/.

Citizens Advice. (2022b). Direct Discrimination. *Citizens Advice*. https://www.citizensadvice.org.uk/law-and-courts/discrimination/what-are-the-different-types-of-discrimination/direct-discrimination/.

Equal Rights Advocates. (2019). KNOW YOUR RIGHTS AT WORK: Gender Discrimination at Work. *Equalrights.org*. https://www.equalrights.org/issue/economic-workplace-equality/discrimination-at-work/.

Grant, A. [@AdamMGrant] (2019, June 20). Leaders don't claim to be victims of injustice. They take responsibility for stopping injustice. Leaders don't attack the powerless. [Tweet]. *Twitter*. www.twitter.com/adammgrant/status/1144975373920194566?lang=en.

Great Schools Partnership. (2015). Hidden Curriculum. *The Glossary of Education Reform*. https://www.edglossary.org/hidden-curriculum/.

Healthline. (2019). How to Identify and Manage Workplace Bullying. *Healthline*. https://www.healthline.com/health/workplace-bullying.

NSPCC. (2021). History of child protection in the UK. *NSPCC*. www.learning.nspcc.org.uk/child- protection-system/history-of-child-protection-in-the-uk.

Verge Safety Barriers. (2018). Negligence in the workplace: Consequences, rights, and obligations. *Verge Safety Barriers*. https://www.vergesafetybarriers.com.au/negligence-workplace-consequences-rights-obligations/.

XR Training. (2012). What is Safeguarding? [Video]. *XR Training*. https://www.youtube.com/watch?v=CcwdbmDl7x8.

Chapter Seven

Total Inclusivity is a journey that we, as individuals, must commit ourselves to. There are no quick fixes, and it won't come about if we leave it to others. Rather, it is about the actions that each of us must take today which will help to co-create a more equitable tomorrow for all of us.

A key aspect of that future must be individual wellbeing.

In terms of education, 'wellbeing' has emerged as a powerful term and concept not just in the West but globally. Over the past decade, there has been increased discussion, and concern, about student wellbeing, happiness and self-confidence, with links drawn between these factors and subsequent academic achievement. This has often felt like an 'either/or' conversation – with student wellbeing and student achievement appearing to occupy different discursive spaces within schools and in the minds of school teachers and leaders. The COVID-19 pandemic, however, has steered this conversation in a more positive direction, because it has forced schools to place the physical and emotional wellbeing of their students (and staff) at the centre of what they do.

While the pandemic has pushed student and educator wellbeing to the fore of educational discussion, the downside is that the same pandemic has placed us all under more stress and pressure than ever before. We are undoubtedly living in emotional and anxious times, and schools have an increasing role in helping learners acquire the knowledge and skills to manage these stresses and develop the confidence and emotional resilience to lead a happy and healthy life (Street, 2018).

With the emotional turmoil experienced by so many young people, combined with the added (and ever-increasing) educational and societal pressures to be successful, how do we best help our students?

To answer that question we need to first understand what wellbeing is.

DOI: 10.4324/9781003231233-9

UNPACKING WELLBEING

Wellbeing is concerned with us 'being well', and this has many different facets depending on what is important to us. In this sense, wellbeing is much like a fingerprint – something that we all share but that we all experience differently. Martin Seligman, founder of the Positive Psychology movement, provides a useful framework for unpacking how we can be well. Seligman (2012) noted that wellbeing isn't one single thing (nor does it have one simple definition) but is rather made up of five different elements: (1) positive emotion, (2) engagement, (3) meaning, (4) positive relationships and (5) accomplishment.

The 'meaning' element highlights the importance of the social side of wellbeing, and this is where total inclusivity becomes closely aligned with wellbeing. To be Totally Inclusive is to create spaces where everyone belongs and where everyone is treated with dignity. As Street (2018) explains:

> Definitions of wellbeing that focus too narrowly on individual characteristics are in danger of becoming meaningless theories of everything. Wellbeing is not simply about individual expressions of thoughts, feelings and behaviours; it is not an isolated or solitary pursuit. It is just as much about the connections we form with others, the tasks we pursue and our wider sense of the world.

Street contends that all too often when a student is distressed at school, we tend to focus on how we can support and address this at the individual level. Instead, she encourages us to ask the question of not what the individual can change to help themselves but, rather, how we can create a healthier environment for all.

A key factor that is often missing from discussions around wellbeing is diversity, equity and inclusion. We are a part of the world around us and cannot separate ourselves and our sense of 'being well' from our wider communities, friendships and relationships. This is why Total Inclusivity must focus not only on the individual but also the broader concept of 'us'. Whilst there is important work currently being done by many groups and individuals in this area, discussions highlighting **the intersecting nature between identity, social justice and wellbeing** are yet to catch up.

Wellbeing concerns our 'being well' as social beings, not just human beings. It is about creating and reacting to a social context in a healthy and positive way. Ultimately, lasting wellbeing and happiness have far less to do with any aspect of our individual functioning than we might like to think, and far more to do with the spaces between us.

(Street, 2020)

For example, when it comes to LGBTQ+ and gender-non-conforming students, research tells us that, globally, these students experience a higher rate of bullying and discrimination in schools (UNESCO, 2016). This links to our previous discussions in Chapter Three on stereotypes, as gender and sexuality-based violence occurs in schools where discriminatory views and norms towards LGBTQ+ individuals are upheld or left unchallenged. Additionally, almost 50% of LGB students and more than 60% of trans students are bullied in schools in the UK, and approximately 50% of LGBT students hear homophobic slurs on a frequent basis (Bradlow et al., 2017).

Further to this, a review of bullying in UK schools by the Education Policy Institute (2018) stated that "girls, ethnic minorities, those with special educational needs and disabilities, and LGBTQ+ pupils more likely to experience discriminatory bullying". The report highlighted how different marginalised groups may experience bullying differently and explained that whilst male students are more likely to be hit or threatened, female students were more likely to experience more covert forms of bullying such as isolation and rumour-spreading. Additionally, it noted that almost 60% of girls aged 13 to 21 have experienced some form of sexual harassment in the past year, and approximately 70% of females aged 16 to 18 hear gendered insults on a regular basis. The report also highlighted that 'ethnic minority pupils' experienced significantly more bullying in UK schools.

The simple fact is that students' (and staff members') wellbeing and sense of self are significantly impacted by their ability to be who they truly are and to express their intersectional identities without fear. Whilst wellbeing is a complex concept with multiple layers, we contend that one of the most powerful ways in which wellbeing can be placed at the centre of school is through the creation of Totally Inclusive spaces.

TOTALLY INCLUSIVE SPACES

As we now explain, there are four key considerations and ways in which you can help create Totally Inclusive spaces, and these involve (1) visibility and representation, (2) curriculum and resources, (3) empowering students through providing spaces and (4) spaces for staff support.

Visibility and Representation

Visibility and representation matter in so many different ways. If we think back to when we were at school, were there teachers that looked like us? Were there teachers who expressed diverse sexual orientations or gender identities? Were there teachers who we could relate to and identify with?

Wellbeing is to belong, and to belong is to know that we're not on our own, isolated or dismissed. We are social creatures, and we are always looking to our environment for reassurance that we will fit in and be accepted.

As educators, it is important to be reflective of what the environment we are in tells our students about the world. After all, schools are a microcosm of the wider world – the only difference is that it is within our powers to shape the school environment more directly and intentionally!

Representation matters. We cannot overlook the importance of our students being educated by people that have similar identities to them and who have lived experiences that they can relate to. According to research by the Yale Child Study Center, teachers that share similar racial identities to their students demonstrate an increased empathy towards them (Hathaway, 2016). All of our students deserve to be in an environment where they have adults who can truly empathise with them - but if we do not make efforts to ensure that our staff body is representative of the students that we teach, this is unlikely to be the case.

So how can we increase visibility? Well, in lots of different ways, but we'll share a few ideas with you here.

One colleague reported to us that they were surprised at the power of wearing a Progress Pride flag on their school lanyard. They explained:

> The week I started wearing my new Pride Progress flag I had a couple of students ask me about it, who I actually have never really had a conversation with outside of talking about the subject that I teach. One Year 7 student came up to and asked, "Is that a pride flag? What do the different colours mean?" After I explained each section of the flag, that the brown and black part is to represent "People of Colour", and what the intersex part of the flag means, the student then asked me, "What is your sexuality?" Caught off guard and wondering whether it was perhaps quite an intrusive question, I decided instead to welcome their curiosity and explained that I was gay and that I was married to another teacher in the school. Rather than feeling embarrassed or self-conscious, I came away realising how important it was to normalise these conversations with students. A badge is such a simple thing, but I was really taken aback at how many students noticed it and how many were curious and wanted to find out more.

Representation has the power to create a 'new normal'. It is not simply about the representation itself, but how this increased visibility creates new messages, stories, and experiences for students that become a part of how they understand and interpret the world. One of the authors reflected on being an openly lesbian teacher in an international school:

> My wife was recently working on a project in which she was sharing some of her experiences as an openly gay PE teacher, and this got us thinking about some of the questions that we often ask ourselves relating to our sexuality and its impact or interpretation by others. Questions that we feel you wouldn't ask yourself if you identified as a cisgender, heterosexual individual, and in particular the question of whether or not being openly gay unintentionally makes us 'role models' for LGBTQ+ students. At times I still find myself selectively expressing my 'gayness' in a professional setting, and when I married my wife I found that I was forced to confront my sexuality in ways I hadn't necessarily done so before. I felt a shift in which it became unacceptable

to let people assume (or not correct the assumption) that we were friends. At times this has made my life easier. But it has also made me sad that I was accepting of my relationship not being viewed or valued in the same way as a heterosexual relationship. Somehow I became complicit in the devaluing of my relationship and the love that I had for my then girlfriend and now wife. As a result of these feelings, I would question my worthiness or eligibility as a role model for young people who may also be questioning their identity or sexuality.

In discussions with other educators about these views, the author found that many LGBTQ+ teachers also felt that they often had to suppress or hide their sexuality in a professional setting for a wide range of reasons. Some feared backlash from the school or parents, whilst others just didn't feel comfortable being open with their sexuality. Representation in and of itself can be incredibly complex because there are human beings at the heart of it, with different experiences and understandings about different aspects of their identities. This is why, as we will shortly come on to explain, spaces for staff support and expression are so important.

Having your identity validated, particularly after years of repressing one's identity, can be incredibly powerful. As one teacher explained to us:

My first teaching post was in a UK inner-city school, overwhelmingly made up of white students and staff. I was the only Black (male) teacher, and as such I was treated as something of an anomaly and curiosity. Fortunately (or not), I also happened to be the PE teacher so my Black identity fitted the dominant stereotype of all Black people being good at sport – though this alone didn't spare me the racist comments and innuendos, from both colleagues and students. I managed to acquire some validation of my personal and professional self through the success of our sports teams – but there was no chance of me being considered for a more senior position and my working life was not that pleasant. I was seen as the Black PE teacher and that was it. And then an amazing thing happened – the city education authorities (who to be fair were quite enlightened on racial matters) appointed a female Black headteacher. Overnight my status and relationship to the school changed. Not only were there now two Black teachers in the school;

the school was led by a Black woman. No longer was I the outsider (well, not as much as I had been), and at least I could now see a career pathway open up for me. That was a big turning point in my sense of wellbeing at that school and actually in my career in education from then on.

Visibility also goes beyond representation. To borrow from Rudine Sims Bishop's (1990) concept of "windows, mirrors, and sliding glass doors", schools, staff and curriculum must not be a 'mirror' reflecting back the views of dominant cultures. Schools must also act as 'sliding glass doors' where teachers and students can see and understand the world from the perspectives of non-dominant cultures. In this sense, representation isn't just about providing students with the opportunity to be taught by people with similar identities; the presence of staff from non-dominant cultures also enables those from dominant cultures to better understand the world as it truly is and not simply the world that is uncritically reflected back at them.

Curriculum and Teaching Resources

Curriculum and teaching resources are an incredibly important way in which we can signal that our classrooms are safe spaces for all. They can, and should, be shaped to reflect the world that we live in, and that our students will enter. There has been some excellent work in recent years by collectives such as ODIS (Organisation to Decolonise International Schools), and Stonewall, to help ensure that we are conscious about how what we teach includes or excludes.

The decolonisation of the curriculum movement (as previously discussed in Chapter Four) can be traced back to 2015 when, at the University of Cape Town, South Africa, a statue of colonialist figure Cecil Rhodes was removed. This instigated student movements and calls to action around the world to fight for structural change, first in universities and later in schools (Shay, 2016). The decolonisation movement encourages educators to question the lens through which knowledge is being taught and consider whose views and experiences are being represented. It is often very difficult to understand the impact of colonisation of the curriculums that we are teaching, as the curriculum and the social forces that have shaped them are the water that we are swimming in (Sensoy and DiAngelo, 2017). Many of us, particularly white educators, may never have felt the need to question what we were taught, and what we now teach, because the curricula we have experienced have always represented us. However, the same cannot be said for many of our students and colleagues.

At an international school, a colleague shared: "In our upcoming Grade 4 unit of inquiry about Exploration, I do not want it to be about dead white guys." She went on to collaborate with her teaching team to co-create a dynamic unit that led 9- to 10-year-olds to critically explore the impact of colonisation on Indigenous communities. Students made conceptual connections regarding fear and control between colonisers, the wealthy, police brutality and political figures such as Donald Trump. In addition to this, they also made connections after exploring multiple explorations that the colonised experienced struggle that still exists today in marginalised communities such as people of colour, women, people with disabilities, homeless people and more. A shift in curriculum design brought deeper understanding and cultivation of socially responsible citizens.

In addition to recognising the need to decolonise the curriculum that we teach and critically examine the pedagogies that we use, the intentional choice of teaching resources that we use is extremely important. One colleague shared with us:

> We are so grateful to our daughter's school that the students get a chance to read books with characters and families just like them. As gay parents, we have been concerned about our daughter being treated different because her family looks different, and we didn't know how she would cope when other kids started to ask questions. When my daughter brought home a book that had a family with same-sex parents in it I was so delighted, as it meant that all of the other students my daughter was in class with would also learn about families like ours and see them as 'normal'.

One further way that curriculum is important is in the opportunity it provides for our students to learn empathy (Huang, 2021). Learning empathy must go beyond 'walking in someone else's shoes' and should arm students with a better understanding as to why it is important for them to care. In order to ensure positive social change, students need to truly understand the depth and breadth of racism, homophobia, transphobia, sexism and ableism. Students should be exposed to both local and global issues and supported to make connections between these and wider societal structures and inequalities. One international school colleague explained to us:

> I am so grateful that we had the opportunity to collaborate with a fantastic organisation that supports migrant communities. Working in an international school, I think it is essential that students understand the social and political issues on their doorsteps, as they will be the ones helping to shape the future. One of our students that attended a trip to visit this organisation told us that it had a profound impact on them. They'd lived and grown up in this country, and yet had very little knowledge of the issues faced by migrant populations prior to this. When they came back to school, they remained in contact with the organisation, helped with fundraising efforts, and are hoping to go back to volunteer again individually. It was genuinely transformative for them.

Empowering Students through Providing Spaces

Young people are more politically aware than ever, and they have a fundamental role to play in shaping the future. More than this, young people create and instigate change. There are many ways in which we can empower young people, and an example of one such student initiative is Gender-Sexuality Alliances (GSAs).

Gender and Sexuality Alliances (GSAs)

GSAs (formerly known as Gay-Straight Alliances) are "student-run organizations that unite LGBTQ+ and allied youth to build community and organize around issues impacting them in their schools and communities". GSAs have evolved from being a safe space for LGBTQ+ young people (particularly at the secondary school level) to groups that are striving for social change on a range of different issues including racial, gender and educational justice. GSAs can have a combination of three different roles which include social (meeting other LGBTQ+ youth), support (to discuss a wide range of issues facing LGBTQ+ youth) and activism (students help lead campaigns and events to raise awareness and improve climates in their school) (GSA Network, 2021).

Having a safe space or affinity group for (especially marginalised) students to connect, discuss issues and receive peer affirmation is important for wellbeing. A recent study by Poteat et al. (2020) found that involvement in GSAs had the ability to decrease symptoms of depression and anxiety, and members who discussed mental health topics reported reduced mental health concerns. Furthermore, this study highlighted how groups that come together to discuss and address issues related to equity and justice, in turn, positively impact on members' mental health. Representation and empowerment matter!

When it comes to the importance of student equity groups, one high school student shared with us:

> It's really important to have a space where we can talk about things that are kind of taboo to talk about with teachers or parents. Being a part of a student group has helped me because it's made me realise how many other students feel the same way that I do at times, which is pretty alone. It's also helped to develop more confidence to talk about issues that are impacting me both personally, as well as bigger issues that are going on in the world such as racism, homophobia and transphobia. We never really had anything like this before, but in the last year the student equity group at our school has really grown, and more and more people are having open discussions about their own experiences of discrimination.

Some schools may choose to have an equalities group, which has a very similar remit to GSAs in terms of bringing students together to educate and challenge discrimination pertaining to protected characteristics. This includes addressing issues of racism, islamophobia, transphobia, homophobia, sexism, ableism and mental health discrimination.

The important thing is that these spaces are created by students for students. Students should be predominantly responsible for creating the vision for the group, naming it, diversifying it and running it. Leaders and teachers can help guide but more often than not, it is the students that will be educating us!

Staff Support

An often-overlooked part of inclusion and social justice work is supporting staff. Not always, but very often, it will be staff from marginalised groups that will be heavily involved in or leading work towards

Total Inclusivity. That is not to say that work around diversity, equity and inclusion is or should only be done by marginalised groups. It is vitally important that the school is compelled by moral purpose to help those most affected by systemic prejudice and discrimination and to engage **all** staff in this work. Until all are on board, support is needed. As one colleague shared with us:

> I am tired. I am tired of being the only one that seems to say anything. I am tired of putting myself at risk by sharing my thoughts and by fighting for what I think is right. I am also tired of the gaslighting and being made to feel like I am imagining the problems that I am highlighting. Recently, a member of senior management that has very little knowledge of DEIJ issues (and admits just as much) had the audacity to tell me that I need to be careful not to be too 'single-minded'. I often hear sentiments like, 'Well, we all have opinions, who's to say yours is right?' or 'We have to consider both sides.' I find it infuriating when I experience the exact discrimination that I'm fighting to change for my students.

When asking this individual whether there has been anything that has helped them process these types of behaviours, they explained that sharing their experiences with other people who may have experienced similar treatment had been particularly important. This leads us to the importance of affinity groups. Affinity groups are usually where members of a shared identity (based on race, gender identity, sexuality, disability, etc.) engage in discussions related to their identity. Whilst there are times where it is better to have a discussion with a range of identities, there are also instances where separation can be valuable. The organisation Racial Equity Tools (2020) explains that when it comes to racial equity work, there is work for white people and people of colour to do both together and apart. Working within your own racial/ethnic group can enable different discussions to take place. For example, an affinity group for educators of colour can provide space to openly talk about the impact of racism and create a space for individual and collective healing and liberation. An affinity group for white educators can provide time and space to understand and reflect on the prevalence and impact of white privilege and culture. These affinity groups may take place on a local, or international, scale, and social media is a helpful place to search for these opportunities.

Providing space for reflection and healing is vital to educator well-being. As Nunana Nyomi (2020) states in his article 'International education perpetuates structural racism and anti-racism is the solution', one of the key steps for schools to take in advancing their anti-racism work is to affirm that Black Lives Matter. Nyomi highlights the fact that racism is transnational and that the impacts of racialised violence are felt far beyond US borders. Schools and institutions that are slow to acknowledge both the traumatic impact of the racialised violence flooding students' (and teachers') social media feeds and that fail to issue statements of solidarity are harming our schools. We must remember that silence on the issues of social (in) justice that are felt within our school communities is a deliberate act, one that is actively choosing to not support all members of our school communities.

CONCLUSION

This chapter has highlighted that wellbeing is inextricably linked to the spaces we inhabit. In this sense, wellbeing is not something which is a singular 'problem' for the individual, wellbeing intersects with our individual identities and wider issues of social justice. The school climate and work culture, value system, and representations of diversity especially across teaching and leadership teams, all contribute positively or negatively to the individual wellbeing of both staff and students. If there are wellbeing issues apparent in your school look first at the school culture, not at the individual.

Whilst wellbeing remains a complex concept, one of the key ways that wellbeing can be placed at the heart of our schools is through the intentional creation of Totally Inclusive spaces. In order to do this, greater visibility and representation in our schools must be encouraged and celebrated. Our curriculums and teaching resources must be updated to authentically value the diversity of identities, cultures and languages that exists in the world. Most important, we need to find ways to empower our students and staff. We can achieve this by providing opportunities (through GSAs and affinity groups) for greater exploration of the parts of their identities which undoubtedly impact their sense of wellbeing.

CHAPTER SEVEN: REFLECTION, GUIDANCE AND COMMITMENT

Reflections: What does wellbeing mean for you, personally and professionally? How do you distinguish between feeling under pressure at work but nevertheless content to feeling under siege at work and most definitely not content? Is your job in education enabling a feeling of wellbeing in you, or is it making you unwell? If you can reflect on how your own sense of wellbeing is enabled or diminished in your school, then you can begin to reflect on how your colleagues may also be experiencing the same (or different) emotions and responses. This is a good starting point for addressing these issues.

Guidance: As with much of the guidance offered in this book the most positive approach is to begin talking about these issues, openly and without fear of consequence. Wellbeing should not be an aspiration in a school, it should be treated and considered as an entitlement. Don't hide behind a school culture or climate which privileges silence and 'just getting on with the job'. That neither helps you, your colleagues, or, most important, your students. Initiating a 'wellbeing' conversation in the staffroom might be a good start. It can then broaden out to include all aspects and all members of the school community.

Commitment: Schools must be safe places for all, where diverse identities are protected, valued, and nurtured. Make a commitment to ensuring that is the case in your school. Don't be silent, don't accept the status quo; don't brush aside situations which undermine or damage a person's wellbeing. Be a positive contributor, an agent of change.

REFERENCES

Bishop, R. S. (1990). Mirrors, windows, and sliding glass doors, *Perspectives*, 6(3): ix–xi.

Bradlow, J., Bartram, F., Guasp, A., & Jadva, V. (2017). School Report: The experiences of lesbian, gay, bi and trans young people in Britain's schools in 2017. *Stonewall.* www.stonewall.org.uk/sites/default/files/the_school_report_2017.pdf.

Education Policy Institute. (2018). Bullying: A review of the evidence. *Education Policy Institute.* www.epi.org.uk/publications-and-research/bullying-a-review-of-the-evidence/.

GSA Network. (2021). What is a GSA club? *GSA Network.* www.gsanetwork.org/what-is-a-gsa/.

Hathaway, B. (2016). Implicit bias may help explain high preschool expulsion rates for black children. *Yale News.* www.news.yale.edu/2016/09/27/implicit-bias-may-explain-high-preschool-expulsion-rates-black-children.

Huang, J. (2021). AIELOC: Community Visioning September 2021. *AIELOC.* www.drive.google.com/file/d/12cXQMoboPS2ncNgBM_1bor00rYDUGgPP/view.

Nyomi, N. (2020). International education perpetuates structural racism and anti-racism is the solution. *Council of International Schools.* www.cois.org/about-cis/news/post/~board/perspectives-blog/post/international-education-perpetuates-structural-racism-and-anti-racism-is-the-solution.

Poteat, V. P., Calzo, J. P., Yoshikawa, H., Lipkin, A., Ceccolini, C. J., Rosenbach, S., O'Brien, M. D., Marx, R. A., Murchison, G. R., & Burton, E. (2020). Greater engagement in Gender-Sexuality Alliances and GSA characteristics predict youth empowerment and reduced mental health concerns, *Child Development,* 91(5): 1509–1528.

Racial Equity Tools. (2020). Caucus and Affinity Groups. *Racial Equity Tools.* www.racialequitytools.org/resources/act/strategies/caucus-and-affinity-groups.

Seligman, M. (2012). *Flourish: A Visionary New Understanding of Happiness and Well-being.* New York: Atria books.

Sensoy, Ö., & DiAngelo, R. (2017). *Is Everyone Really Equal?: An Introduction to Key Concepts in Social Justice Education* (2nd ed.). New York: Teachers College Press.

Shay, S. (2016). Decolonising the curriculum: it's time for a strategy. *The Conversation.* www.theconversation.com/decolonising-the-curriculum-its-time-for-a-strategy-60598.

Street, H. (2018). *Contextual Wellbeing: Creating Positive Schools from the Inside Out.* Subiaco, WA: Wise Solutions Pty Ltd.

Street, H. (2020). The Social Side of Wellbeing – an extract from Contextual Wellbeing By Dr Helen Street. *LinkedIn.* https://www.linkedin.com/pulse/social-side-wellbeing-extract-from-contextual-dr-helen-schools/.

UNESCO. (2016). *Out in the Open: Education Sector Responses to Violence based on Sexual Orientation and Gender Identity/Expression.* Paris: United Nations Educational, Scientific and Cultural Organization.

Leaders and Leading
Chapter Eight

Are leaders born or made? What does it mean to be a leader? And what is the role of leadership in creating a Totally Inclusive School? Ask any group of educators these questions and you will get different answers. This chapter shares what we believe 'being a leader' means, the role of leaders and how leveraging power and building alliances can help overcome resistance.

Your relationship to leadership may vary, but it is our belief that leadership is a skill that every individual can develop. If you are an educator in a school, then leadership is undoubtedly a key part of your professional identity. Why? Because the job of every educator is to lead, influence and have an impact on others, whether they be the students in your classroom, the teaching team you belong to or your colleagues. In a learning ecosystem, every person's actions impact the health of the school environment they inhabit.

So, what kind of leader do you want to be?

If the notion of leadership scares you it could be that you are uninterested in having a title or that you are wary of power. However, being a leader is not a title that a school gives to you; it is an offering that you give to the school (Wambach, 2019). Whatever your position in a school, you can lead, and you do not have to wait for permission to do so. Irrespective of your personal comfort levels when it comes to leadership, think more about power as having power **with** others to have a positive impact rather than having power **over** others as a manager (Kise and Watterston, 2019).

It is our belief that every member of a Totally Inclusive School community should be encouraged to think as a leader, whether in a formal or an informal capacity. Think about, for example, who you would turn to if you were looking for a resource to support a student with dyslexia? Or when looking for lesson resources that contain greater diversity and representation? Who would you go to if you

DOI: 10.4324/9781003231233-10

were looking for anti-bias, anti-racism learning and teaching strategies? For resources about dyslexia, there might be several colleagues you could turn to – perhaps the special educational needs coordinator or academic support team or a colleague that you know who recently took a course in this area. In seeking diverse resources, you may know of colleagues who have used these within their own lessons and units previously. For anti-bias, anti-racism strategies, it might be the school counsellor who has training and experience with culturally responsive teaching and teaching for equity. These educators have a reputation; it is what they are good at and where they have influence and impact. None of them may be senior leaders, managers or administrators (principals, heads of schools or board members), and yet they are leaders within their respective areas or specialisms. They are leading from where they are.

THE ROLE OF LEADERSHIP

To create the culture and conditions necessary for all to take on leadership roles, leaders lead by establishing a shared purpose, encouraging shared responsibilities and building leadership capacity in the learning community.

—Brown (2018, p. 6)

Establishing the 'shared purpose' required to turn our Total Inclusivity vision into a reality is no easy feat, especially when we are living in what are commonly described as volatile, uncertain, complex and ambiguous times. The more complex society becomes, the more sophisticated leadership needs to be (Fullan, 2001). To achieve Total Inclusivity in schools we are tasked with furthering change and addressing problems that often do not have easy answers.

Tackling discrimination and inequitable infrastructure is complex, full of paradoxes and dilemmas. Many will expect leaders to provide answers to these complex issues, and this expectation is untenable. The best one can hope for is that through their leadership more good things will happen than bad, resulting in fewer disruptions to change efforts, less disheartenment, fewer isolated interventions and greater use of resources (Fullan, 2001).

And who makes these good things happen? Teachers!

Teachers are the single most influential component of an effective school (Marzano, 2007). Without teachers, leaders will be left leading a school building full of administrative and facility staff and with a community waiting to be served. Students are the core of what teachers do, and must be a part of a leader's focus. Effective teachers equal effective learning and teaching. It is a professional, collaborative community of educators who have the power to co-create a Totally Inclusive School. With this in mind, a school leader's key task is to develop collective teacher efficacy. Collective teacher efficacy is the shared belief of educators in their ability to positively affect students, and this has been found to be the most impactful factor towards student success (Waack, 2018; Hattie, 2010).

Bandura's social cognitive theory declares that individual and group beliefs influence the motivation, commitment and creative approaches that people embody when approaching tasks. To address inequities in schools, leaders need to adopt an agentic perspective toward human development, adaptation and change. Having an agentic perspective means that leaders view individuals as self-organising, proactive, self-regulating and self-reflecting, not merely spectators of their own behaviour (Bandura, 2006). Therefore, leaders must work in partnership with other community members to support teachers to build relationships with students and guide them to develop the mindsets, knowledge, skills and understandings they will need to be successful (as guided by a school's mission and vision). Fostering a culture in which staff believe that they can work together to actualise a Totally Inclusive School is vital.

Raising collective teacher efficacy will help to accelerate your diversity, equity, inclusion and justice (DEIJ) agenda (Goddard et al., 2015). For example, a common theme that arises in affinity group spaces for educators (Black, Indigenous and People of Colour [BIPOC] groups, LGBTQ+ groups, etc.) is frustration. Often, they express that the urgency they feel for DEIJ initiatives to be adopted and implemented is not equally shared by their colleagues or leadership team. In order to comprehensively move DEIJ initiatives forward, schools need the commitment and engagement of all community members. When only individuals or smaller groups display the understanding and drive required for change, early advocates can become disillusioned. Therefore, a leader's role is to motivate all members of their community to move forward as a collective.

One might ask, what are schools invested in? Quite simply, it is learning. For every learner to have a successful experience they need a sense of safety and belonging. This is acquired by being able to identify themselves and one another through meaning-making of the world around them (Radd et al., 2021). We must count all students and adults as learners in a school community, and to further that learning, we need socially responsible leadership. Radd et al. (2021, p. 49) share that when developing equity-focused leadership it is important to:

1. recognise that the way things are can be changed and
2. be alert to the challenges you will face as you attempt to make that change.

Therefore, working towards a shared understanding of how the normalised culture of our schools impacts how students see themselves and continue to evolve their own identities is crucial. In other words, our students' experiences of school have an impact on their understandings of race, gender, sexual orientation, class, disability, age, religion, linguistic diversity and more (Radd et al., 2021).

When co-constructing a Totally Inclusive School, a leader needs to be able to recognise and differentiate between problems that are solvable and polarities that need to be managed. The following figure provides information that helps educators leverage polarities (Figure 8.1).

A leader not only needs to be able to manage polarities, but they can also leverage both sides when taking on a DEIJ challenge. Sometimes, polarities that appear to be pitted against each other are actually opportunities to be leveraged. For example, the language of instruction versus the multilingualism polarity. Instead of pitting these as forces in opposition with each other, we need to frame this as language of instruction **and** multilingualism. In many schools across the globe, learning English is prioritised, and in schools with English as the language of instruction, there are leaders who see speaking

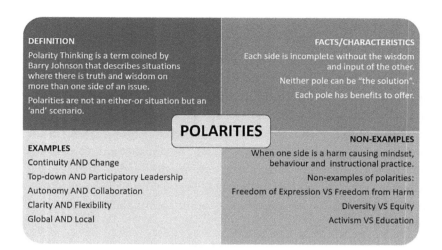

Figure 8.1 Explanation of Polarities using a Frayer Model template
Source: (based on Kise, 2014)

another language at school as detracting from the goal of learning English. Leaders who support English-only policies and hire teachers favouring native English speakers are not leveraging multilingualism, and by 'solving' the problem (according to their perception), they are in fact asking members of their community to leave their language profiles at the door. Instead, leaders who leverage polarities will enrich their communities by valuing diverse languages and cultures. Good school leaders can see complex topics as manageable polarities rather than problems in need of random solutions (Abrams, 2019) and work to resolve them in ways that benefit their students and communities.

When it comes to polarities within schools, a common concern shared with us by several educators is the way that issues are addressed in which one side is a position that causes harm to another. For example, in one instance, a Korean student claimed that a white American student had been racist towards them and used inappropriate language. Rather than acknowledging the student's concerns, the teacher involved with the complaint instead minimised the impact of the comments that had been made, which included jokes about "Kung Flu" (in relation to the COVID-19 pandemic). The white teacher sided with the white student and suggested that the Korean student should try to understand "the other side of the story". This is a problem. One side of this story causes harm to another.

In another example, following a parent complaint, a school that had previously not specified gender on single-stall toilets decided to allocate all toilets within their school building as either male or female. As a result, members of the student body who identified as trans or non-binary were left confused and upset about which toilets they should use. To have toilets that were not gender-specific did no harm to cisgender students, as they could choose to use the gendered toilets that already existed on the campus. But for transgender and intersex students, the removal of the genderless toilets caused very real harm.

These situations are not polarities to be managed because there is no wisdom or truth when one side is racist or transphobic. They reveal a polarisation of beliefs where intercultural understanding is not present, and a lack of clarity exists in the school regarding what is acceptable. A crucial role of school leaders therefore is to clarify a school's vision, code of ethics and the written and unwritten rules that cultivate a sense of belonging and community.

LEADING WITH AUTHENTICITY

People don't care how much you know until they know how much you care.
—Brown (2018, p. 179)

What is your purpose as a Totally Inclusive leader? Why are you passionate about these values? What story can you tell that illustrates your commitment to this work?

If you can answer these three questions, then you have the foundations to lead with authenticity. And these are answers that are unique to you. One of the authors of this book is passionate about being a Totally Inclusive leader because she herself experienced racism in schools as an Australian migrant growing up in a dominantly white suburban Sydney. During this time she was held back from mainstream classroom activities for speaking English with an accent, having travelled to Australia from Malaysia, where she was born. This has made her passionate about anti-racism, promoting multilingualism and ensuring that no child suffers marginalisation in school. In addition to this, her eldest son has an intellectual disability, and this has given her insights into the challenges faced by families navigating school systems that are not always designed to provide accessibility for learners with neurodiversity. Her story has shaped her purpose and passion and driven her motivation to commit to this work.

Another of the authors of this book identifies as a gay woman. In a professional context, she has often been fearful to share her identity with colleagues and students and worried about the reaction of parents and the wider school community. And yet, when she encounters students who are questioning their own identities, who are struggling to come to terms with their sexuality, she feels the need to speak up and speak out, to live her truth, to work to create safer spaces for those students. She recognises the need for them to see an adult who is comfortable and accepting of themselves and who will affirm and celebrate who they are. This has provided her with the motive to work towards Total Inclusivity. This is her why.

If you reflect on your own "why" you will discover the values that are most important to you. As Abrams (2019, p. 23) explains:

> Before beginning to determine how to implement an initiative, it is essential for your credibility that you are able to articulate how the project aligns with your values. After all, beyond all the hype or the noise, the research and the recognition, one must know what one stands for. What are your beliefs? What values do you want to make sure undergird your work? It will feel inauthentic if you cannot state how this initiative aligns with your values.

A value is a way of being or believing and is what we hold as being most important. Our behaviours are driven by our values, whether we want them to or not, and therefore, we must take care of our intentions, words, thoughts and behaviours (Brown, 2018). As leaders, our actions are constantly being interpreted by others. Every teacher experiences this as they notice their students adapting to their routines and ways of working. Students watch, and absorb, our actions and our inactions. How you are perceived by others in the community depends on the image you project (whether consciously or not).

One way of thinking about your imprint as a leader is by considering 'Impression Management'. This is defined by Whitehead

(2006, p. 51) as "maintaining a personal/public image and identity performance which corresponds with the positive culture and values of the organisation/school". If you work in a place where the culture and values align with your own, then your behaviour (and personal 'image') is more likely to parallel the public image of your school. However, in adopting 'impression management', we risk curbing our authentic selves to suit archaic perceptions of what a school leader should look like. We should instead focus on viewing our 'brand' as a direct result of our actions.

Our brand is the sum of how we are perceived by others, and we have no control over others' perceptions. We can only control our own actions and, in doing so, influence how we are perceived. Understanding our brand identity helps us understand how our behaviours are being interpreted. At times we may not like what we hear about our brand, or ourselves, and this should invoke deep reflection about how our behaviours and impact may not be aligning with our self-perception or the image we aspire to project. These questions, adapted from Cass and Stone (2017) may help you define your brand:

1. Why does your school/DEIJ initiative exist?
2. What is your/your school's story?
3. What challenges are you helping your school solve?
4. Why do others trust you/your school?
5. Who do you trust and look up to?
6. What five characteristics would you use to describe yourself/your school?
7. What is your brand voice and how do you communicate this?

In our communications as a leader, we must share our purpose, morals and ethics. It is one of the key ways we gain trust from those we are leading. How we communicate in conversations, emails, newsletters and reports matters. The coherence between what we *say* we will do and what we *actually* do defines us in the eyes of others.

LEVERAGING POWER

Power is one of the most misunderstood concepts in the study of social, organisational and political dynamics. It is not a material construct but a psychological one. It covers a range of complex social dynamics and can be wielded in both positive and negative ways. Why is power important? Well, if you are intending to bring about any type of change in a school, you'll need the power to do so. You'll also need to be aware of the way power dynamics will shape and influence your journey towards Total Inclusivity.

Power exists in different forms, and depending on our positionality, power dynamics can shift back and forth. Positionality is how our identity markers afford us social position and power (CTLT Indigenous Initiatives, n.d.). For example, as a Chinese Australian living in Berlin, one author is positioned as both a migrant and belonging to a race that is well represented by the global majority but underrepresented in Germany. This not only gives her power in some spaces but also renders her without positionality in other spaces. In the school that she has worked at since 2005, she has positionality as a senior member of staff through her position as curriculum coordinator and as a member of the primary school's leadership team. In recognising positionality, we must also be aware that complex power dynamics are at play that are determined by our intersectional identities, diversity, resources, personality, social skills, connections and more.

School structures are reflections of society's values and norms. Within society, there are some groups in schools that have power, and others that do not. Schools with hierarchical structures resemble caste systems. This is where certain individuals or groups may have (or not have) respect, status, honor, attention, privilege, resources, benefit of the doubt, human kindness and/or dignity based on their perceived positionality (Wilkerson, 2020). Some leaders uphold hierarchical structures in schools in order to maintain positionality and privileges and to uphold dominance and power. According to Wilkerson (2020, p. 72),

> [r]ace and caste are not the cause and do not account for every poor outcome or unpleasant encounter. But caste becomes a factor, to whatever infinitesimal degree, in interactions and decisions across gender, ethnicity, race, immigrant status, sexual orientation, age, or religion that have consequences in our everyday lives.

Leaders striving for Total Inclusivity need to have a critical understanding of power, positionality and power dynamics and reflect on the degree to which these influence the everyday interactions and actions taking place within their schools. They should be acutely aware of how these power dynamics can either expand differences between people or be leveraged to close the gap. Here are some reflection points related to power dynamics, and considerations for how you can wield your power and positionality:

- Do you have power over a person/ group or power with a person/group?
- Do you have the power to increase differences or celebrate differences?
- Do you have the power to show bias or promote equity?
- Do you have the power to violate rights or to create safe and secure environments?

What happens when people do not have power? They likely feel uneasy because they cannot make decisions or act with autonomy. They may feel as though they have no control. This undermines a person's identity and sense of self-worth. Therefore, as leaders, we need to start by valuing all identities and respecting the diversity present in our school communities. We need to develop our understanding of power dynamics and consciously shift power by empowering and emboldening (student and staff) learners.

Individual leaders can be powerful, and so can groups. Both can not only be powerful to bring forth an initiative but can also be powerfully wrong (Fullan, 2001). Therefore, we need multiple systems in place to give us perspective. For example, are we gaining information from different community members? Are we building relationships across various groups? Is our messaging building trust across the school?

Consider how you can share and distribute power across your school community so that your students, staff and community members become co-creators of Total Inclusivity. This could be through, for example, the creation of student-led diversity and equity groups who engage in issues of social justice and are empowered to affect change both within their schools and the wider communities they inhabit.

OVERCOMING RESISTANCE

Laura Morris is standing in front of her school board. A teacher in Loudoun County, Virginia, US for 10 years, this is, for her, the end. She can take no more.

> You have made your point. You no longer value me, or many other teachers you've employed in this county.... School board, I quit. I quit your policies, I quit your trainings, and I quit being a cog in a machine that tells me to push highly politicised agendas on our most vulnerable constituents – the children ... these political ideologies do not square with who I am.
>
> (as cited in Kilander, 2021)

And just what has pushed her, and many other teachers in Loudoun County, over the edge?

A new transgender inclusion policy being enacted in their schools, stating:

> Transgender students should be allowed to use their chosen name and gender pronouns that reflect their consistently asserted gender identity... staff should use those pronouns as well. Staff or students who intentionally and persistently refuse to respect a student's gender identity by using the wrong name and gender pronoun are in violation of this policy.
>
> (as cited in Kilander, 2021)

If you decide to lead your school towards Total Inclusivity, you are going to meet resistance. You may lose some otherwise professionally competent teachers who do not like the idea of gender-neutral toilets, gender pronouns, critical race theory, LGBTQ+ student groups or having to attend training that explores white privilege, unconscious bias or intersectionality.

You may lose some friends and colleagues. There will be times you'll feel vulnerable, isolated, exposed and unsure.

But as one parent who supported the very same policy put it:

> I am encouraging you all to support policies that are inclusive of transgender students and to show your support for transgender students

and transgender faculty. This isn't pseudoscience, this isn't some sort of ideology. This is people's lives. This is civil rights.

(as cited in Kilander, 2021)

You don't need to be leading a school towards Total Inclusivity to recognise you'll meet resistance. If you are a leader, resistance is something you must learn to live with – it will never disappear completely.

Resistance to equity work comes in various forms, including emotional reactions and moral resistance (Radd et al., 2021). Resistance can arise perhaps because the shifts we are asking for are pushing them out of their comfort zones or felt to be 'too challenging'. However, if initiatives do not challenge people enough, then maybe what we are asking for is not transformative enough to be worth our time. Finding that 'just-right' initiative doesn't exist, as all community members will arrive at the work from multiple entry points. We need to remind ourselves that we do not own or control other people's emotions, and it is not a leader's job to do so (Brown, 2018). When forced out of one's comfort zone, fragility can manifest in various behaviours, such as being intentionally spiteful, reactive, petty or engaging in sabotage behaviours. As a leader, regardless of the behaviours directed at you, you must strive to be objective when hearing feedback and not allow your ego to detract from your mission.

One way in which leaders can overcome resistance is to build alliances across the school community and beyond. Identifying advocates for DEIJ and early implementers of new initiatives will be crucial for sustainable success. If you are a head of school, it is imperative that you build alliances with key players on your school board. Without support from your governing body, you will be unable to secure the commitment necessary to fund and accelerate positive change within your school. Community members to build alliances with include parents, students, leadership teams in senior or middle leadership, support staff and, last but not least, teachers. These people can then help with expanding and strengthening relationships, transform how power can be used, integrate personal experiences to systems/trend data and assess the credibility of data gathered.

125 Leaders and Leading

Finally, any school leader looking to align with Total Inclusive values and eventually develop a school which can be readily identified as Totally Inclusive in every aspect of its operation will need to build strong and self-supporting teams within their community. Such teams should exhibit the following characteristics:

- Shared leadership across teams (disrupting hierarchical power reliant structures)
- Clear goals, roles, responsibilities and purpose related to the school vision
- Provide opportunities for growth, learning, mistake making and coaching support

Such teams are created when there is a clear and mutually agreed alignment on the direction of the school. This requires leaders to instil a shared belief in the vision of Total Inclusivity and make clear the role of every individual in getting there.

IMPACT OF LEADERS

Leaders in schools have a crucial role to play. If you are a senior leader stepping into a head of school role, then you are taking ownership of the school that you have inherited. This includes all the wrongs that may have occurred before your time. For example, at one international school, an Instagram account started by alumni and students to share stories of racist behaviour at the school went viral. Members of the senior leadership team had two choices: try to shut it down or enter into a process of deep reflection as a school and take ownership of the behaviours that happened at the institution. Over a year after this incident, the school has now become an international school leader for DEIJ initiatives. Senior leaders at the school engaged in reconciliation behaviour, taking ownership of the school they inherited.

When students speak, we should always listen.

As Wilkerson (2020, p. 16) states, "We are the heirs to whatever is right or wrong with it. We did not erect the uneven pillars or joists, but they are ours to deal with now."

As leaders we are not going to always get it right. So, we need to normalise mistakes. When doing so we need to be grounded by our ethics.

Fullan (2001, p. 19) writes that "moral purpose cannot just be stated, it must be accompanied by strategies for realizing it, and those strategies are the leadership actions that energize people to pursue a desired goal".

These strategies need to consist of clear purposes, consistency across systems and flexibility to adapt to changing needs.

Whether you hold a formal leadership position or not, you are strongly encouraged to speak truth to power and move forward intrepidly. This will be seen as support for Total Inclusivity and an understanding that you'll purposefully move from intention to implementation to impact.

SEVEN TIPS FOR LEADERS

1. Share your vision for Total Inclusivity. You cannot create a Totally Inclusive school on your own. You'll need alliances (with teachers, parents, students, governors), you'll need effective teams at all levels of the organisation and you'll need advocates.
2. Consider the timing and urgency of the changes you need to make. Some will need to be prioritised over others. Some may be quick and easy to action; others will require longer-term planning and ongoing reflection and evaluation.
3. The vision of Total Inclusivity belongs to every member of your community. Distribute power. Ask them to embrace the process as co-creators of Total Inclusivity.
4. Recognise the difference between 'intent' and 'impact'. Your intentions may be good and honourable, but how you implement them may result in a very different, sometimes negative, impact. If this happens, take action to repair any harm that has been caused.
5. Value the individuals you work with. Listen to their perspectives. If disagreement makes you uncomfortable, reflect on why that is and give space to revise your understandings and beliefs.
6. Meet people where they are on their own Totally Inclusive journey. Find the balance between challenge and comfort.
7. Commit fully to your shared vision of Total Inclusion. You must 'walk the talk' and back up your words with action.

CHAPTER EIGHT: REFLECTIONS, GUIDANCE AND COMMITMENT

Reflections: Consider the following questions: What power do you have to influence equity? How could you leverage your positionality and power to make a difference, and address diversity, equity, inclusion and justice in your school?

Guidance: Leadership is always a work in progress. Set high standards for yourself, morally and ethically, but accept that sometimes you'll get it wrong. When those times arise, and they will, forgive yourself while also reflecting on what you can learn from the experience.

Commitment: Plan ahead now to address the resistance you will inevitably face. Consider initiatives that could be used to address this resistance, for example, hosting listening circles where cross sections of community members are invited, for example board members, teachers and parents.

REFERENCES

Abrams, J. (2019). *Swimming in the Deep End: Four Foundational Skills for Leading Successful School Initiatives* (p. 23). Bloomington, IN: Solution Tree Press.

Bandura, A. (2006). Toward a Psychology of Human Agency, *Perspectives on Psychological Science*, 1(2): 164–180.

Brown, B. (2018). *Dare to Lead: Brave Work. Tough Conversations. Whole Hearts* (pp. 6, 179). London: Ebury Publishing.

Cass, J., & Stone, E. (2017). 7 essential questions to define your brand. *Just Creative*. https://justcreative.com/7-essential-questions-to-define-your-brand/.

CTLT Indigenous Initiatives. (n.d.). Positionality & Intersectionality. *Indigenous Initiatives*. https://indigenousinitiatives.ctlt.ubc.ca/classroom-climate/positionality-and-intersectionality/.

Fullan, M. (2001). *Leading in a Culture of Change* (p. 19). San Francisco: Jossey-Bass.

Goddard, R., Goddard, Y., Sook Kim, E., & Miller, R. (2015). A theoretical and empirical analysis of the roles of instructional leadership, teacher collaboration, and collective efficacy beliefs in support of student learning. *American Journal of Education*, 121(4): 501–530.

Hattie, J. (2010). *Visible Learning: A Synthesis of Over 800 Meta-analyses Relating to Achievement*. Oxon: Routledge.

Kilander, G. (2021). Teacher cries as she quits in front of Virginia school board considering more inclusive transgender policy. *The Independent*. www.independent.co.uk/news/world/americas/teacher-quits-virginia-school-transgender-b1900965.html.

Kise, J. A. G. (2014). *Unleashing the Positive Power of Differences: Polarity Thinking in Our Schools*. Thousand Oaks: Corwin Press.

Kise, J. A. G., & Watterston, B. K. (2019). *Step in, Step up: Empowering Women for the School Leadership Journey*. Bloomington, IN: Solution Tree Press.

Marzano, R. J. (2007). *The Art and Science of Teaching: A Comprehensive Framework for Effective Instruction*. Alexandria, VA: Association for Supervision and Curriculum Development.

Radd, S. I., Givens, G. Z., Gooden, M. A., & Theoharis, G. (2021). *Five Practices for Equity-Focused School Ladership*. Alexandria, VA: ASCD.

Waack, S. (2018). Collective Teacher Efficacy (CTE) according to John Hattie. *VISIBLE LEARNING*. www.visible-learning.org/2018/03/collective-teacher-efficacy-hattie/.

Wambach, A. (2019). *Wolfpack: How to Come Together, Unleash Our Power, and Change the Game*. London: Piatkus.

Whitehead, S. (2006). 'Contingent masculinities: disruptions to 'man'agerialist identity', in S.M. Whitehead (ed.), *Men and Masculinities: Critical Concepts in Sociology* (Vol. II, *Materialising Masculinity*). London: Routledge.

Wilkerson, I. (2020). *Caste: The Lies That Divide Us* (pp. 16, 72). New York: Random House.

Total Inclusivity and Your
Institution
Section III

The Total Inclusivity Continuum for Schools

Chapter Nine

So far, we have focused on understanding ourselves and key concepts and have considered the importance of working towards a Totally Inclusive School. In this and the final chapter, we shift our focus to your institution and consider tools to help us move from theory to practice. An anchoring self-assessment tool is a continuum that outlines what schools look like at different stages of development. Schools need a tool like this to help them identify their current stage of development and to envisage the next steps needed as they aspire to become Totally Inclusive.

INTRODUCTION TO THE CONTINUUM

The Continuum on Becoming a Totally Inclusive School is designed to help individuals and institutions identify their stage of development. The descriptors capture key behaviours and mindsets commonly found or lacking at each stage as well as institutional systems and structures that are characteristic of certain points of growth. It aims to be a formative tool that outlines foundational aspects to consider when developing and assessing a school. Using this continuum will help educators pinpoint growth initiatives and to scaffold learning opportunities. A breakdown of each stage is provided as well as ideas for possible next-step actions.

Each school will have multiple entry points in this assessment tool. Depending on a school's construct, it may already be founded on similar principles, and hence, the development stage may not begin at Stage One. Also, a school may identify with more than one stage as there may be inconsistent practices across an institution. This is not uncommon. Ultimately, it is the dialogue, critical thinking and reflection that are important, and this tool aims to be a stimulus for constructive conversations that lead to action. The discussions that

DOI: 10.4324/9781003231233-12

arise about why multiple perspectives exist will bring to the surface tensions, issues to address and initiatives to implement.

It is important to recognise that while schools may aspire to progress over time, multiple factors may impede development and schools may find that they regress. A continuum is most effective in recording growth, stagnation or regression over time. A plan to revisit the continuum at regular intervals signals a commitment to long-term institutional change. How often this process should be revisited depends on the duration of strategic initiatives, and this will differ from school to school.

BALANCING PERCEPTIONS AND EVIDENCE-INFORMED ASSESSMENTS

Whilst individual educators may find reflecting on this continuum useful, it is most impactful if teams of educators are able to have dialogue about the descriptors and how they relate to their school's culture and context. Involving students, parents, governing body members and other community members will enrich reflections. Educators' experiences, expertise and professional judgements are valid forms of evidence that have been historically undervalued compared to quantitative or qualitative data. Perceptions from professional experiences can be powerful contributions towards identifying aspects of school development that warrant further investigation.

One way to approach the continuum is to gather overall data first, and to use these results to determine the school's stage of development. Data collection is a complex process and can be informative depending on the tool used and the purpose for collection (see also Chapter Ten).

There are two starting points for using the continuum:

1. Starting with more generic data collection, then reflecting on this continuum using analysed information to identify a school's stage **or**
2. Starting with reflecting on the continuum and then identifying specific areas to collect data on depending on needs.

Either way, it is recommended that diverse representation of individuals from multiple areas of the school be involved and that the focus on growth is both individual and institutional (The Leadership Academy, 2021).

INSTITUTIONAL PHASES OF DEVELOPMENT

The continuum describes characteristics of schools that are **inequitable** at one end of the spectrum and that are **Totally Inclusive** at the other end. As schools journey towards Total Inclusivity, they must be **reflective** in order to be **transformative**. These phases of development are not always linear and schools aspiring to make progress need to engage in honest and deep reflection processes. Schools also need to recognise the iterative nature of this work.

Table 9.1 shows the continuum in its entirety. As you engage with the continuum for the first time, consider its components and the descriptors of what each phase typically looks like. What do you notice? You are likely to make connections with your own school's behaviours/mindsets and systems/structures or be thinking of situations that are familiar to you. What is resonating with you? As you read on, what clarifications are you hoping to have about the continuum? Keep these wonderings in mind as you engage with the rest of the chapter.

INDIVIDUAL DEVELOPMENT OF MINDSETS AND BEHAVIOURS

A school at a beginning stage of growth sees diversity as a deficit. As schools move away from a deficit mindset the overall culture becomes more tolerant of differences. When individuals within an institution deepen their understanding of diversity, equity, inclusion and justice (DEIJ), they engage in recognising and reflecting on the inequities that exist in their current institution. This knowledge positions individuals to make informed decisions and help a school develop their Totally Inclusive identity.

It is vital that individual or group motivations are identified before using the continuum. Commitment from senior leadership and a school's governing body to a long-term, strategic growth is essential for bringing self-identified initiatives forward. Use of the continuum should be just one step to take in an ongoing journey. Middle leaders and influential members of the community who perform informal leadership roles are resources to optimise when using this assessment tool. It may be that the continuum is used for individual reflection or utilised by a group of advocates who have been identified as champions to drive initiatives and accelerate organisational change. Supplementary materials to support individual and group use can also be found in this chapter's Reflection, Guidance and Commitment section.

Table 9.1 Continuum on Becoming a Totally Inclusive School

INEQUITABLE <==> REFLECTIVE <==> TRANSFORMATIVE <==> TOTALLY INCLUSIVE

	1. Discriminatory	2. Exclusive	3. Symbolic Change	4. Embracing	5. Structural Change	6. Totally Inclusive
	An Inequitable Institution	A Tokenistic Institution	A Contradictory Institution	A Diverse Institution	A Transforming Institution	An Equitable & Just Institution
Behaviours / Mindsets	• Intentionally and publicly excludes or segregates by an identity marker such as, but not exclusive to, race, gender, sexual orientation, class, disability, age, socio-economic status, religion and language ability. • Upholds a dominant culture that perpetuates a patriarchal, colonial status quo throughout the institution. • Dominant cultural views embedded in curriculum, values and teaching approaches. • Students/staff voices are largely invisible in decision-making	• Tolerant of a limited number of 'token' representations of diverse identities allowed in who have a 'proper' perspective and credentials that are a 'good fit'. • Learning spaces to explore diversity, equity, inclusivity, justice and anti-racism not prioritised and/or discouraged. • Continues to uphold a dominant cultural, patriarchal, colonial status quo throughout the institution. • Often declares, "We don't have a problem." • Engages issues of diversity and social justice only on 'club' members' terms and within their comfort zone.	• Expanding view of diversity includes other socially oppressed groups. • Carries out intentional inclusiveness efforts, e.g recruiting 'someone of colour'. • Learning spaces are one-off opportunities and limited to surface-level knowledge with low expectations for transfer or application. • Students/staff engage in planned actions to promote Total Inclusivity and justice. **But …** • "Not those who make waves" and challenge practices. • Majority of individuals remain relatively unaware of continuing patterns of privilege, paternalism & control.	• New consciousness of systemic inequalities and understanding of barriers to valuing diversity, equity, inclusivity, justice and anti-racism. • Awareness of and checks implicit bias and develops clear lines of accountability to all oppressed communities. • Student/staff voices being heard and accountability to oppressed and/or disenfranchised individuals and/or communities developing. • Ongoing actions and commitment to the work recognise that mistakes, a growth mindset and accountability are essential for progress.	• Intercultural diversity becomes an institutionalized asset. • Commits to dismantling racism, discrimination, prejudice in the wider community, and builds clear lines of accountability to all oppressed communities. • Redefines and rebuilds all relationships and activities in society, based on Totally Inclusive commitments. • Student/staff voices, including those in historically oppressed and/or disenfranchised groups, are intentionally integrated into decision-making processes. • Sense of accountability is evident and a growth mindset drives progress.	• School's life and culture reflect full participation and shared power with diverse racial, sexual, gender, cultural and economic groups fully participating and represented equitably. • Members across all identity groups are full participants in decisions that shape the institution, and inclusion of diverse cultures, lifestyles, and interest. • A sense of restored trust, community and mutual caring. • Student voices and learner agency continually nurtured to promote Totally Inclusive practices.

diversity seen as deficits <==> tolerant of differences <==> recognising and reflecting on inequities <==> reacting and rebuilding towards inclusivity <==> diverse, equitable, inclusive and just

Systems / Structures					
• Institutionalised discrimination, evident in policies and practices, decision-making on multiple levels, such as selective admission of students and hiring practices. • Power, privilege and advantages of dominant group(s) substantiated in policies and practices. • Leadership teams decision-making processes covertly and/or overtly maintain discriminatory practices. • Individuals, groups or school lacks accountability for inequitable and unjust practices.	• Uses politically correct public policies in communications whilst systems, decision-making and culture remain unchanged, discriminatory and/or inequitable. • Cultural norms, policies and procedures of dominant culture viewed as the 'right way' and 'business as usual' • Student/staff complaints of discrimination, past or present, dismissed and/or rationalised to protect the school's reputation. Their opinions sought but mostly not listened to. • Volunteer(s) advocate for initiatives but is largely seen as an additional add-on that is likely unpaid.	• Makes official policy pronouncements regarding any combination of the following: diversity, inclusivity, equity, justice, anti-racism. • Adopts policies due to legal requirements and/or as a reactionary measure. • Resources (time, money) given to individual/team leading the work. But … • Little or no contextual change in culture, policies, and decision-making. • Actions reflect one-off performative allyship that is not sustained over time • New diverse recruits expected to assimilate into organizational culture.	• Sponsors advocates, training and programs related to Total Inclusivity. • Develops a school identity as a Totally Inclusive institution • Actively recruits, promotes and creates opportunities for historically oppressed individuals/groups. • Leadership team intentionally works towards overcoming resistance at different levels and works towards Total Inclusivity. But… • Institutional structures and culture that maintain white, patriarchal power and privilege still intact and relatively untouched. • Continued resistance by some people remains unaddressed at different levels of the school	• Commits to the process of intentional institutional restructuring, based upon Total Inclusivity values, ethics, aims and objectives. • Restructures all aspects of school life to ensure full participation from a diverse landscape of individuals and communities, including their worldview, language, culture and lifestyles. • Implements structures, policies and practices with inclusive decision-making and other forms of power sharing on all levels of school life. • Institution acknowledges and takes responsibility for historical harm to move forward.	• School community works effectively and systematically in ensuring a Totally Inclusive mission, structure, constituency, policies and practices. • Allies with others in combating all forms of social oppression. • Actively works in larger communities (regional, national, global) to eliminate all forms of oppression and to create intercultural organizations. • School undertakes regular and systemic assessment of strategic actions to evidence growth and ensures all aspects of the school community maintain alignment with these aims.

<== Performative Allyship ==>   <== Commitment to Institutional Transformation ==>

Adapted from Bailey Jackson Chapter Nine: Theory and Practice of Multicultural Organization Development, The NTL Handbook of Organization Development and Change: Principles, Practices, and Perspectives, 2014.

THE SIX STAGES OF DEVELOPMENT

The continuum consists of six stages of development. As a school aspires to become an equitable and just learning community there must be continual action as individuals and the institution learn together. Like climbing or descending stairs, it requires effort, movement and, most important, a clear vision of an end destination. To help educators and schools achieve this ideal state, each of the following stages has been described in detail. We also provide a table for each stage which further describes typically found policies, procedures and practices.

The six developmental stages are:

1. Discriminatory – An Inequitable Institution
2. Exclusive – A Tokenistic Institution
3. Symbolic Change – A Contradictory Institution
4. Embracing – A Diverse Institution
5. Structural Change – A Transforming Institution
6. Totally Inclusive – An Equitable and Just Institution

A school at the first three stages of development may be engaging in what can be classified as acts of performative allyship. This may look like schools beginning to reflect on their practices and not yet committing to dismantling historically discriminatory practices or committing to superficial change in order to intentionally maintain the status quo. Through reflective inquiry, an institution can build collective capacity as the learning community strives towards sustaining authentic allyship. When schools truly commit to institutional transformation, actions taken will shift from being performative tasks to collaborative co-practices.

The main characteristics of the six stages of development are categorised into behaviours/mindsets and systems/structures. The systems/structures typically found in the school's policy and infrastructure, as well as leadership qualities and actions, are described at each stage. Common challenges are outlined, as well as suggestions for initiatives to develop at certain stages.

It is essential to recognise that each school is different and making connections to the descriptions and advice in this chapter to one's own context is critical to success. Each of the tables in these stages includes starting points for reflection. Contextualising is an opportunity for interactive inquiry that can be supported by the process outlined in supplementary material 9.3 – the Continuum Deep Dive template. This template can be used to explore all six stages and to identify possible next-step initiatives.

STAGE 1. DISCRIMINATORY – AN INEQUITABLE INSTITUTION

A discriminatory school is one that overtly excludes cross sections of identities that do not fit into the school's idealised 'norm' and brand and are committed to maintaining a dominant group's power and privilege (Jackson, 2014). Depending on where the school is situated legal obligations vary, and schools may be engaging in more covert ways to discriminate. For example, a discriminatory school may seek to hire 'native speakers' and certain passport holders, but not declare this in their job posts.

Mindsets at this stage of development centre on the behaviours of a dominant cultural group and the feelings of people that belong to or uphold this group's status quo. This mindset reveals itself when individuals dismiss divergent thinking, engage in tone policing and silence voices that question policies, procedures and practices. It can also manifest in behaviour that gaslights another's experience (i.e. attempting to manipulate them into believing their thoughts or perceptions about something are wrong). Implicit biases may drive discriminatory behaviour, although some actions can also be intentionally made to exclude non-dominant identities. Retribution, implicit or explicit, against those who speak up about inequities may be weaponised at this stage, for example using employees' contract renewals or potential dismissal as punitive measures to silence dissenting voices.

It is difficult for any school leader, teacher or member of the governing body to openly admit that their school is functioning at this Discriminatory Stage. Therefore, if your self-assessment landed you at this stage of development, you must be intrepid enough to stand up for what matters to you; courage, like a muscle, can be trained (Kergall, 2020). If you are a leader in a school, the responsibility for the well-being, safety and growth of each student is your primary duty of care. A fear of failure and a lack of accountability holds individuals back at this stage of development. But failure is not a problem so long as we learn from it (Patel, 2021). If your instinct is to turn away, or brush aside and subsequently uphold inequitable policies and practices, then this chapter will challenge you. If your intention is to learn from mistakes so as not to repeat them in the future, then it is vital to engage in actions that will help expose understanding gaps, provide new perspectives and elevate reflection to help shape subsequent actions.

Realising your school is functioning in this stage can invoke strong reactions: denial, retreat, anger, shame or guilt. Schools in denial may ignore, dismiss or debate the need to prioritise DEIJ values. Leaders may well claim to uphold 'school traditions' without reflection on how they are discriminating against cross sections of identities (past and present). If this stage is not seen as a wake-up call leading to learning and action, then the school is likely to be proud of its identity, believing its success lies in its existing values, however exclusive, discriminatory and unjust these practices are. Failing to evolve out of this stage and having no plans to address DEIJ issues reveals an individual and institution's core values. Given the current climate and awakening to decolonise, be anti-racist and Totally Inclusive by design, dismissing this call to action will lead individuals or institutions to obsolescence and ultimately failure. In a school that has values aligned with Total Inclusivity's aims, the dignity and rights of all will be an unchallengeable priority and not up for debate.

To progress out of this stage, it is important to recognise practices and infrastructure for what they are and how they are resulting in negative experiences that cause harm and reflect on one's moral purpose as an educator. Understanding the impact inequitable school experiences have on historically oppressed groups or individuals is vital. As a first step towards positive change, leaders need to acknowledge and take responsibility for systems they may have inherited, designed and/or upheld. This will require a fearless stance to face inequities, lean into discomfort, manage risks and take courage to stand up for what matters (Kergall, 2020).

Examples of next-step initiatives include the following:

- Introductory workshops to raise levels of understanding about power and privilege, culturally responsive classrooms, safeguarding and safe reporting pathways, courageous conversation protocols and more

- Implicit bias training that includes exploration of microaggressive behaviours and how they marginalise cross sections of the school's population
- Implement a survey tool such as the Intercultural Development Inventory (IDI) to provide profiles of individuals' orientations toward difference (IDI Inventory, 2020) (See Chapter Ten.)
- Analyse current policies using a DEIJ lens and identify all terms and concepts requiring shared understanding.

To move away from being an inequitable institution, shifting an individual's mindset from seeing diversity as a deficit towards acceptance of difference is the priority. For some, it may mean taking a step towards acceptance by being tolerant of differences. For others, reaching acceptance and adaptability can occur at a more accelerated pace (Table 9.2).

STAGE 2. EXCLUSIVE – A TOKENISTIC INSTITUTION

An Exclusive institution seeks to uphold a dominant group's supremacy by maintaining power structures and privileges (Jackson, 2014). This tokenistic stage is one in which differences are recognised and 'model minorities' are welcomed into an exclusive 'club'. This is limited to people who are perceived as being an ideal 'cultural fit' and who are able to assimilate into the dominant culture's behavioural norms. In this stage individuals, consciously or unconsciously, support institutional structures that uphold a dominant cultural, patriarchal, colonial status quo. In an Exclusive Stage, an 'old boys' club' can still thrive because although they are maintaining an inequitable status quo, they are not breaking any written rules, making it difficult for Total Inclusivity advocates to challenge powerful leaders. While differences may be acknowledged at this stage, stereotypical beliefs about identities can underlie an 'us versus them' mentality that leads to prejudiced behaviour (IDI Inventory, 2020). Behaviours are likely to be defensive in nature with individuals critical of another culture while finding their own superior. Individuals from historically marginalised groups may also be prejudiced against their personal inherited cultural values by perceiving the dominant culture they are exposed to as

Table 9.2 Discriminatory Stage – Main Characteristics and Examples of Practice

	Continuum descriptors	Practices from the learning community
Behaviours/Mindsets	• Intentionally and publicly excludes or segregates by an identity marker such as, but not exclusive to, race, gender, sexual orientation, class, disability, age, socio-economic status, religion and language ability. • Upholds a dominant culture that perpetuates a patriarchal, colonial status quo throughout the institution. • Dominant cultural views embedded in curriculum, values and teaching approaches. • Student/staff voices are largely invisible in decision-making.	**What educators may say** – "I don't see colour. All lives matter." – "Why does everything have to be about _____ (race/sexual orientation/etc.)?" – "I don't need this training, it doesn't apply to me." (Radd, et al., 2021) – "Couldn't they have said that in a more respectful way?" – "I was brought up to not talk about race. It's a taboo topic and not relevant to the success of my students." (Moule, 2012). – "Could it be that they meant _____ instead?" – "If we use the term feminist or anti-racist, don't you think it will scare people off?" – "That's just kids being kids. It was not meant that way. It's typical teenage/immature/child behaviour." (Lindsey, et al., 2019) – "I don't think they were offended by it, _____ laughed about it too, so it must not have been _____. Let's not make a big deal out of it." – "That is racist against white people…"

Systems/Structures

- Institutionalized discrimination, evident in policies and practices, teaching and decision-making on multiple levels, such as selective admission of students and hiring practices.
- Power, privilege and advantages of dominant group(s) substantiated in policies and practices.
- Leadership teams decision-making processes covertly and/or overtly maintain discriminatory practices.
- Individuals, groups or school lacks accountability for inequitable and unjust practices.

Policies and Infrastructure

Child protection policy may be in place; however, safeguarding practices for all in the building is not. This results in behaviours that violate individuals' rights and safety. Incidents are largely unreported.

Hiring practices attract a narrow scope of candidates and leadership's hiring choices show affinity bias towards people within their known circles or with backgrounds similar to their own.

Overemphasis in the school calendar of Christian cultural festivals such as Christmas and Easter even though the school is non-secular and the community is diverse.

Decision-making acquiesces to what is perceived as parental expectations, and this is often cited as to why practices need to remain as they are.

DEIJ values do not underpin design and implementation of the school's action plan, policies and curriculum.

superior. For example, local students attending international schools will likely encounter individuals or groups speaking critically about the country or culture they are living in or are from and may absorb this into their own thinking. This could be, for example, through hearing their (non-local, expatriate) teachers express frustration with 'the way things are done' in comparison with an idealised view of their own country's systems (typically holding Western systems in higher esteem). Over time, students may begin to believe these perspectives to be true.

Actions taken by educators at this stage can be performative one-off celebrations of diversity that are enacted within people's comfort zones (Jackson, 2014). However, everyday practices in the classroom and interactions between different community members remain inequitable. For example, educators may be unsure of how to adjust their instructional practices or curriculum materials to meet the needs of diverse learners. Classroom cultures may reflect conformity and compliance as opposed to environments where diverse ideas are safely shared. Students from non-dominant groups are more likely to be punished for behaviour and their performance assessed more harshly due to likeability and attribution biases. Advocates trying to move initiatives forward are largely seen as add-on agenda items being ticked off a list of to-dos rather than seen as valuable assets. Overall, there is a feeling that since there are a handful of people with visible, diverse identities succeeding in the school this is evidence that 'we don't have a problem', and this is used to justify maintaining the status quo.

Schools at the Exclusive Stage will have a 'business as usual' culture. There may be developments related to DEIJ; however, these are token efforts that can be classified as minimum gestures to appease. Beliefs about power and privilege, and the myth of meritocracy drive decision-making in classrooms, meetings, hiring and at the senior leadership level. Decision-making remains under the control of a powerful, exclusive, self-sustaining group.

Token efforts may be taken to enlist the views of diverse school community members regarding new initiatives; however, this is more to convince others of a predetermined change instead of integrating such voices into the decision-making process. At this stage, leadership is likely to resist liberalising measures by not supporting grassroots initiatives from DEIJ advocates that challenge their own views and mandates. Claims that "parents don't want inclusivity and diversity" originate from attempting to meet perceived expectations of (tax) paying clients in public or private institutions is commonly used as an excuse for inaction. Leaders will present the 'this is what parents want' argument as necessary responses to economic pressures and vital to maintaining school statuses and capital. There may be a DEIJ role, committee or advocate, but that person or group is likely to be heavily micromanaged and given no agency to actually do the work.

Leaders may look to deny opportunities to and exclude those who speak up against injustice. They may appropriate ideas from historically marginalised voices and turn them into their own ideas to suit their agendas. Paternalistic behaviour can also be common at this stage. For example, students and staff may be consulted, although decisions continue to be made executive-order style by senior leaders. Colleagues are seen as not being ready to engage, incapable, uncooperative or not invested in DEIJ, and these are presented as excuses for a lack of commitment to inclusivity initiatives (Radd et al., 2021).

To progress out of this stage, advocates for diversity and inclusion need to be dissatisfied with tokenistic acts and remain forceful when speaking truth to power (Henley, 2019). This means being an upstander, not a bystander, and holding oneself to a higher ethical standard. It is the school that runs the risk of being outdated, not the Total Inclusivity advocate! Without valuing diverse ideas, schools stagnate and will continue to implement outdated learning and teaching practices that are likely to result in failure.

Examples of next-step initiatives include the following:
- Creating opportunities for interactive participation where voices are valued in decision-making and learners (students and adults) can ask questions, make mistakes and co-construct meaning without fear (Right Question Institute, 2020)
- Decentralise decision-making by empowering students and staff to make informed choices
- Facilitate intercultural understanding workshops that shift understanding from token surface-level actions (flags, foods,

fashion, festivals, etc.) to a deeper understanding of how individuals attend to difference (Hall, 1976)
- Create up-to-date and inclusive policies collaboratively with all community members
- Seek the help of a professional who can expand thinking about how to be an effective ally and creator of, liberated communities
- Engage in deep reflection and take actions that have been co-constructed with various community members

To move away from being an exclusive institution, an individual's mindset needs to shift away from being tolerant of differences to one that recognises inequities that exist in schools. For some, it may mean taking a step towards examining their own privileges and power, and for others, it may mean drawing the courage to share stories and speak up against inequities (Table 9.3).

STAGE 3. SYMBOLIC CHANGE – A CONTRADICTORY INSTITUTION

As individual mindsets shift towards recognising and reflecting on inequities, the school is poised to make significant changes to its systems and structures. These may be changes that not all members of the school community are onboard with yet. Whilst there may be an expanding view of diversity, educators at this Symbolic Change stage may be more focused on commonalities, with a belief that focusing on commonalities will bring the community together. Individuals who are from the dominant cultural group may see themselves as globally minded. However, they may be overlooking a deeper understanding of self and interculturalism. Individuals from non-dominant groups will likely go along with the status quo, choosing not to 'rock the boat' although this doesn't necessarily mean that they are in agreement with the norms they have assimilated to (IDI Inventory, 2020). Integration is likely tokenistic (celebrating food, festivals, fashion and fun), for example a curriculum that addresses different identities through special events or following topical trends. While this is a growth step towards Total Inclusivity, valuing differences and developing intercultural skills should be the goal rather than cultural assimilation through commonalities. A saviour mentality may exist in pockets where paternalism drives behaviour. At this stage, individuals

Table 9.3 Exclusive Stage – Main Characteristics and Examples of Practice

	Continuum descriptors	Practices from the learning community
Behaviours/Mindsets	• Tolerant of a limited number of 'token' representations of diverse identities allowed in who have a 'proper' perspective and credentials that are a 'good fit'. • Learning spaces to explore DEIJ and anti-racism not prioritised and/or discouraged. • Continues to uphold a dominant cultural, patriarchal, colonial status quo throughout the institution. • Often declares, "We don't have a problem." • Engages issues of diversity and social justice only on 'club' member's terms and within their comfort zone.	**What educators may say** – " _____ from _____ can't meet these expectations because they don't understand the value of this." – "It was good enough for me and my kids, so teaching this way should be good enough for them." – "Those students/families chose our school, a consequence of this is their need to adapt and assimilate into our culture." (Moule, 2012). – "Maybe there is a reason their history didn't make it into the history books." – "Their parents don't seem to care, so why should I?" (Lindsey, et al., 2019). – "I'm going to call you _____. Your name is too hard for me to say." – "The other kids don't seem to have a problem with the way I teach, look how successful they are." – "They must be so dirty; I mean look at those dreadlocks." – "Our school is diverse. We have Jamal and Abdul in Grade 4; they are black." – "Our colleagues are diverse. We have Ms. Chen who works in the cafeteria and Mr. Ibrahim our janitor."

(Continued)

147 **The Total Inclusivity Continuum for Schools**

Table 9.3 [Cont.]

Continuum descriptors	Practices from the learning community
Systems/Structures	**Policies and Infrastructure**
• Uses politically correct public policies in communications whilst systems, decision-making and culture remain unchanged, discriminatory and/or inequitable.	Change initiatives (if any) are driven by senior leadership appointees who uphold performative mandates.
• Cultural norms, policies and procedures of dominant culture viewed as the 'right way' and 'business as usual'	Inequitable pay gaps exist, especially at the upper levels of leadership. Salary scales are not transparent.
• Student/staff complaints of discrimination, past or present, dismissed and/or rationalised to protect the school's reputation. Their opinions sought but are mostly not listened to.	Systems lacking in areas of response to complaints about discrimination. Complaints may not be recognised or taken seriously and minimised for the greater good of the school's reputation.
• Volunteer(s) advocate for initiatives but largely seen as an additional add-on that is likely unpaid.	Language policy centres on the language of instruction only (most commonly English). A specific dialect and accent are seen as the most desired (most commonly British or American English).
	Curriculum is not representative of the diverse demographics of the whole school constitution of families, educators and the local community.

may also be engaging with learning about their own identities, examining their privileges and recognising their biases. Individuals are also developing advocacy skills as intentionality rises and inquiry-driven learning becomes more invitational and interactive.

At an institutional level, a school engaged in making symbolic changes is seeking to achieve its goals without disrupting pre-existing systems and structures. Although individuals may be gaining new knowledge, understandings and skills to make informed actions, this has not yet become a whole school process. There is goodwill to become a more inclusive institution, but the school acts in contradictory ways. For example, decision-making may still be driven by a mindset that is carefully calculating about how not to make too many waves to offend current families, employees or board members who hold biased prejudices. This stage of development can be filled with inconsistencies. For example, leadership may speak of commitment to initiatives while failing to do the individual work needed to examine their understanding gaps. Leadership may be looking to an individual or a group of educators to lead progress in one area while not intentionally addressing inequitable conditions in another area (Radd et al., 2021). As this stage can be riddled with contradictions, it is especially important that self-reflection as individuals and an institution be focused on identifying examples and evidence of practice that is relevant to one's own school context.

Key challenges include a lack of consistency of practice across the whole school and a lack of follow-through with initiatives. While developmental steps are being taken, it may be unclear who is ultimately taking responsibility for the learning, implementation into practice and accountability measures. Some leadership members may think that it's the responsibility of staff and vice versa, resulting in erratic action-taking. Diversity is seen as a badge to achieve, rather than a resource. Changes to curriculum and instruction happen for a limited time period following on from isolated professional learning opportunities before reverting back to previous routines and habits. Colleagues may be willing to change but are unsure of how to do so and are afraid of making missteps. Fear of backlash is an obstacle to action.

To move out of this stage individuals need to develop their stance as professional inquirers. There is a recognition that what is considered a 'good school' has been centred on an ideal that marginalises those viewed as being the 'other'. Inquiring as to why this has happened may result in symbolic changes but the inherent contradictions within the institution remain.

Examples of next-step initiatives include the following:

- Securing commitment from all members of the leadership team, and governing body, to actively engage in learning about patterns of privilege, paternalism, protectionism and control and how to be culturally proficient and equity-focused
- Creating and committing to sustainable development over time. This should consider possible quick wins, what can be achieved in the medium-term (6–12 months) and what can be achieved over the next years (3–5 years)
- Prioritising and funding initiatives related to DEIJ work
- Establishing ways to measure growth over time and holding all community members to account for planned initiatives
- Greater transparency and democratic decision-making where reasons for decisions provide legitimacy, the process of decision-making is transparent and visible to all. People who are impacted by decisions have opportunities for participation and play a role in the process (Right Question Institute, 2020)
- Work to overcome resistance, overt or covert, by making it clear that a Totally Inclusive, equitable and just institution is the goal. Examples of tools that can be used to achieve clarity include the school's mission, guiding statements, strategic plan of actions, policies, teacher expectations, student behavioural expectations, community agreements, code of ethics, safeguarding policies and more.
- Hold all school community members to account for behaviours and actions that are not aligned with Totally Inclusive beliefs and values.

To move away from being a contradictory institution, a school needs to shift from making surface level symbolic changes and commit to deep institutional transformation. For most schools this is a pivotal stage of development where one goes from recognising and reflecting on inequities, to planning for and taking strategic action. Schools at this Symbolic Change stage are poised for accelerated progress as long as the leadership team supports the learning community across this tipping point (Table 9.4).

Table 9.4 Symbolic Change Stage – Main Characteristics and Examples of Practice

	Continuum descriptors	Practices from the learning community
Behaviours/Mindsets	• Expanding view of diversity includes other socially oppressed groups. • Carries out intentional inclusiveness efforts, e.g. recruiting 'someone of colour'. • Learning spaces are one-off opportunities and limited to surface-level knowledge with low expectations for transfer or application. • Students/staff engage in planned actions to promote Total Inclusivity and justice. **But …** • "Not those who make waves" by challenging the status quo. Majority of individuals remain relatively unaware of continuing patterns of privilege, paternalism & control.	**What educators may say** - "Learners have the same opportunities, so if they work hard they will be successful." This mindset upholds the myth of meritocracy. - "I really don't see colour. I treat all my students the same." (Lindsey, et al., 2019) - "We value different cultures. Every year we have an international day and I love trying all the different foods and seeing the community in clothes from their cultures." - "This focus on DEIJ will pass once our leadership team changes. I've seen initiatives like this come and go." - "I don't have time for this on top of all my other commitments." - "We had unconscious bias training. It wasn't useful for me. I don't see how this is relevant to how I approach learning and teaching." - "We put out a Black Lives Matter statement." - "_____ is in charge of that initiative. I feel that it is well taken care of so I can get on with my teaching." - "I'm worried about what _____ will think about _____ if we change how we teach that."

[Continued]

Table 9.4 [Cont.]

	Continuum descriptors	Practices from the learning community
Systems/Structures	• Makes official policy pronouncements regarding any combination of the following: diversity, inclusivity, equity, justice, anti-racism. • Adopts policies due to legal requirements and/or as a reactionary measure. • Resources (time, money) given to individual/team leading the work. **But …** • Little or no contextual change in culture, policies, and decision-making. • Actions reflect one-off performative allyship that is not sustained over time • New diverse recruits expected to assimilate into organizational culture.	**Policies and Infrastructure** Existing policies revised to make minor changes to reflect DEIJ values. Some changes add value; however, overall little impact or transformation is made. School initiatives show engagement with DEIJ trends that are often perceived as performative and not addressing long-term needs. Reactionary responses dominate decision-making practices. Preventative measures not prioritised. Initiatives tend to be short term. Uses diversity work to enhance the profile of the school. A broader understanding of diversity is under development; however, it is yet to be explicitly defined across the school. Yet to establish sustainable systems, opting for more 'one and done' actions. For example, addressing implicit bias training several semesters ago and not embedding it into new staff induction, resulting in gaps of understanding and transfer into practice. Safeguarding policies deal with overt, dismissable offences; however, reporting of incidents is not forthcoming.

STAGE 4. EMBRACING – A DIVERSE INSTITUTION

At the Embracing Stage, student and staff voices are being heard and this increased input brings enhanced perspectives on how to develop ways to address systemic discrimination and inequities. There is a visible commitment to institutional transformation, and this can be seen in inclusive language being used, in training and curricular programs and in recruitment and retention. There is a majority understanding that success requires ongoing commitment and sustainable actions. All members of the learning community are clear about their behavioural expectations and the school raises awareness through transparent decision-making processes. Different perspectives are seen as an asset that can be harnessed to improve ideas and initiatives.

To take action and build towards inclusivity at this stage, individuals and the school need to recognise that mistakes will be made, people will have uncomfortable feelings and the school will be navigating risks. Families may be resistant to the school's growth and increasingly visible commitments to Totally Inclusive values. At this crucial point, a school could either slip back and regress or react to rebuild and make progress. Regress might look like a return to the status quo or acquiescing to critics in ways that harm cross-sections of the community. As we explained in Chapter Six, developing an understanding that Total Inclusivity is a child protection issue is a fundamental driving force for change. Detractors will find it difficult to argue against upholding children's and human rights.

Learning is messy, and at this stage, the greatest challenge is scaffolding learning and development for all leadership, faculty and support staff. There must also be recognition that inaction towards detractors for their resistance at different levels of the school can be interpreted as condoning behaviour and this lack of leadership undermines morale and progress. As educators embrace differences, they must work extensively to understand key issues and willingly engage with key topics (Radd et al., 2021). This overall commitment will empower the community to translate ideas into practice.

To progress from this stage individuals can take comfort in knowing that they are not alone in this personal and professional work. Educators also have a realisation that white power, privilege and entitlement can be upheld by both oppressors and the oppressed. They embrace their ethical responsibility to be an advocate for social justice for all (Radd et al., 2021). They also either begin to realise that the school is finally in alignment with their goals or that the school's goals towards Total Inclusivity are not in alignment with theirs. If it is the former, then this helps educators renew commitment and motivation. If it is the latter, then individuals begin to recognise that their school's Total Inclusivity mission is no longer in alignment with their own beliefs and this propels resistors to consider moving on as their school continues to bring clarity to DEIJ goals and accountability measures.

Examples of next-step initiatives include the following:
- Differentiated professional learning opportunities across the school related to DEIJ topics with connections to learning and teaching
- Ensuring that there are safeguarding measures for all community members
- Coaching, mentoring, sponsoring and supporting diverse advocates for DEIJ initiatives
- Identifying how to measure impact in specific areas, working out the best method for data collection and establishing baseline measures to track growth
- Continuously engaging in professional inquiry to seek understanding and to co-construct equitable practices
- Engaging in systems and design thinking to spark new ideas and stimulate disruption where needed

To move away from a stage in which one is embracing diversity to one that is undergoing structural change and transformation, individuals and the institution must keep in mind the most marginalised and historically oppressed. This will challenge educators to think of how to meet the needs of those who need it most. As solutions are constructed, and shifts are made to meet those who need the most support, a curb-cut effect will occur. This is when benefits for the most marginalised end up being benefits for everyone (Blackwell, 2017) (Table 9.5).

Table 9.5 Embracing Stage – Main Characteristics and Examples of Practice

Continuum descriptors	Practices from the learning community
Behaviours/Mindsets	• New consciousness of systemic inequalities and understanding of barriers to valuing DEIJ and anti-racism. • Awareness of implicit bias and developing analysis of systemic discrimination and/or inequities. • Student/staff voices being heard and accountability to oppressed and/or disenfranchised individuals and/or communities developing. • Ongoing actions and commitment to the work recognise that mistakes, a growth mindset and accountability are essential for progress.	**What educators may say** – "Can we rename the Christmas holidays the winter/summer break? During that time of the year families in our school also celebrate Hannukah, Kwanzaa and Omisoka, so perhaps winter/summer will be more inclusive." – "I wonder what their linguistic profile is, this may help me scaffold learning for them." – "The more I learn about being an anti-racist, the more I realise that I don't know a lot about our colonial history." – "I realise that I hold assumptions about _____" – "An audit of books in our reading lists showed me that the characters are predominantly white and from male authors." "My student asked, 'Why are all the authors pale, male and stale?'" – "The data tells us _____, so how can we use this to serve our students well?" (Lindsey, et al., 2019) – "Instead of an International Day celebration, can we embed opportunities to learn about our students' cultures throughout the curriculum?" – "How can I do _____ better?" – "What are the different perspectives about this? Which one violates human rights?"

(Continued)

155   **The Total Inclusivity Continuum for Schools**

Table 9.5 [Cont.]

Continuum descriptors	Practices from the learning community
Systems/ Structures	**Policies and Infrastructure**
• Sponsors advocates, training and programs related to Total Inclusivity.	Leadership prioritises DEIJ-related initiatives and integrates them into the school's strategic plans/actions. An action plan gives focus to work (Lindsey, et al. 2019).
• Develops intentional identity as a Totally Inclusive institution.	
• Actively recruits, promotes and creates opportunities for historically oppressed individuals/groups.	Leadership positions in the school are composed of diverse identities. Hiring practices are recalibrated to incorporate DEIJ values.
• Leadership team intentionally works towards overcoming resistance at different levels and works towards Total Inclusivity.	Designated advocate(s) for DEIJ are supported or functioning at the leadership level with time, resources and openly communicated sponsorship.
But ...	Leadership supports learning and teaching by working with families to understand DEIJ values, goals and transformations occurring across the school.
• Institutional structures and culture that maintain white, patriarchal power and privilege still intact and relatively untouched.	Leadership seeks to build and sustain support from the governing body for professional learning and structural changes needed to ensure that systems can be transformed.
• Continued resistance by some people remains unaddressed at different levels of the school.	Data are collected to affirm or challenge assumptions and to gain insights on how to better serve students' needs.
	Voices are sought across a range of community members to inform decision-making. Community viewpoints are carefully considered. Reasons behind decisions are transparently communicated.
	Recognition that institutional structures may need dismantling before they can be rebuilt to serve traditionally marginalised groups.

STAGE 5. STRUCTURAL CHANGE – A TRANSFORMING INSTITUTION

A school in Structural Change is at a transformational stage of redefining itself. It is growing from not just managing diversity to finding ways to evolve into a Totally Inclusive institution (Jackson, 2014). For individuals who have been advocating for DEIJ for a long period of time, the arrival of the school at this stage of development is a welcome affirmation and relief that individual and grassroots initiatives have resulted in structural change.

At this stage, the school's mission, operations and learning and teaching are being examined through diverse perspectives. Educators and learners acknowledge that they are continuously learning about intercultural competence and how their personal identities shape how they deal with difference. The whole community is involved in critical reflection about current practices and in visioning an equitable school and collaborative solution-seeking that is not limited to ideas that fit within the confines of its institutional history. When conflict arises it is seen as constructive to meaning-making and as a progressive step. A school in Structural Change makes bold moves and strives to develop and implement policies, procedures and practices that will result in resources being accessible to diverse learners (Jackson, 2014).

If leaders and educators treat this stage of development as one where revisions to existing structures and systems are enough, then the school may be at risk of regressing or stagnating. The school must recognise that rebuilding is essential to ensure that all learners are included and empowered to thrive. The school must have clearly defined understandings and a common language.

Examples of actionable steps include the following:
- Community visioning to build shared understandings of the DEIJ agenda and what a liberated school looks like, including clear definitions of terms, roles and responsibilities
- Identifying where discrimination continues and addressing it as an institution
- Modelling, valuing and highlighting behaviour and practices that provide learning stories for growth and affirmation that a liberated state is achievable
- Professional learning opportunities led by internal advocates who can contribute to sustaining learning over time in the school

- Continuing to actively reach out to all community members and valuing diverse voices and their contributions to decision-making processes
- Continuing to advocate for and develop new initiatives to meet the needs of marginalised identities
- Continuing to hold individuals to account for their behaviours and the school to account for learners' sense of belonging and success

To move forward from this transformative stage, the whole learning community's collective capacity and mindset needs to reflect the seven I's of Total Inclusivity's Advocacy Stance (see Chapter Ten). The organisation is **intentional** in its actions, **invitational** and **inquiry-driven** when creating learning spaces. The school values **interactive** engagement when collaborating on progressive, equitable solutions. Individuals and systems also address the **interconnectedness** of inequities and respond by dismantling and rebuilding for equity. A school that notices how initiatives have an **impact** will be better positioned to revise initiatives, plans and actions. A steadfast belief that this is the right path will help to counter any challenges that may arise. Any perceived failures should be seen as mere setbacks to overcome. Making bold moves at this stage takes **intrepid** educators and a courageous community built on understanding, shared moral purpose and trust (Table 9.6).

STAGE 6. TOTALLY INCLUSIVE – AN EQUITABLE AND JUST INSTITUTION

A Totally Inclusive, equitable and just institution is where all learners have access to the curriculum in learning spaces that continually strive to eliminate oppression. Educators do this by valuing intersectional identities and by treating each individual as full participants in their learning. Diverse voices are included in school-wide decision-making, and every individual is rightly treated with respect and dignity. With such interactions, individuals build social capital together and trust is a prerequisite for healthy risk-taking (Cox, 1995). With conviction, collaboration and goodwill, both civic culture and school culture thrive.

Table 9.6 Structural Change Stage – Main Characteristics and Examples of Practice

Continuum descriptors	Practices from the learning community
Behaviours/Mindsets	**What educators may say**
• Intercultural diversity becomes an institutionalized asset.	- "Our school stands for this _____."
	- "I find that challenging and I am learning about how to incorporate that into my classroom."
• Commits to dismantling racism, discrimination, prejudice in the wider community and builds clear accountability measures.	- "I have a hunch about _____ and I wonder what my students/ parents/ colleagues think about _____."
	- "Let's slow down and look at this from multiple angles before we proceed." (Radd, et al. 2021)
• Redefines and rebuilds all relationships and activities in society, based on Totally Inclusive commitments.	- "What might be our understanding gaps here?"
	- "I wonder if there is a way to do this that will make it more accessible for _____."
	- "How can we include _____ in this?"
	- "Who haven't we asked about this?"
• Student/staff voices, including those in historically oppressed and/or disenfranchised groups, are intentionally integrated into decision-making processes.	- "What did you mean by that?"
	- "That is not okay. When you said _____, I felt _____."
	- "What you said earlier was _____, because _____."
• Sense of accountability is evident, and a growth mindset drives progress.	- "I'm sorry for _____; I realise now that it _____, moving forward I will strive to _____."

(Continued)

159 **The Total Inclusivity Continuum for Schools**

Table 9.6 [Cont.]

Continuum descriptors	Practices from the learning community
Systems/Structures	**Policies and Infrastructure**
• Commits to the process of intentional institutional restructuring, based upon Total Inclusivity values, ethics, aims and objectives.	DEIJ beliefs and values are embedded into the school's identity and culture, curriculum, learning engagements, teaching strategies, well-being and overall school operations.
• Restructures all aspects of school life to ensure full participation from a diverse landscape of individuals and communities, including their worldview, language, culture and lifestyles.	DEIJ practitioner/team is a part of the leadership team and included in decision-making processes.
• Implements structures, policies and practices with inclusive decision-making and other forms of power sharing on all levels of school life.	DEIJ is a responsibility of all employees, including leadership, support staff and administration teams.
	Data are used to track progress/regress of DEIJ initiatives. Monitoring measures are an integral part of initiatives.
	Learners see themselves represented in resources, in a diversity of identities represented in the teaching staff and professional learning consultants working with the school. Purchasing of resources is data-driven to include diverse representation that reflects the demographics of the school, local and global community.
	Professional learning opportunities offer a deeper dive into specific DEIJ areas. E.g. culturally responsive learning and teaching at a foundational level is an expectation for all, and more specific aspects such as identity-centred learning is a focus for professional inquiry.
• Institution acknowledges and takes responsibility for historical harm to move forward.	Historical practices and institutional injustices of the past are acknowledged and accountability taken for harm caused to marginalised individuals. This recognition is not tokenistic and seen as a step towards healing and growth as an organization.
	Teaching teams are diverse, and contributions to curriculum design include diverse perspectives. In homogeneous teaching teams, educators are conscious of representation matters and engage in ways to expand their viewpoints to inform inclusive curriculum design and delivery.

In this stage, the school's systems and structures serve the most historically marginalised identities, and this is seen as a benefit for all learners. Policies articulate expectations and they don't just sit on a shelf but are alive and kicking through shared understandings that shape and reflect organizational culture. Some may feel frustrated by what they perceive is a slow rate of organizational progress; however, they are sustained by the momentum gained, progress made, accountability measures in place and visible commitment from all. Others may feel challenged by the perceived fast pace of organizational progress; however, they feel supported to develop and have access to multiple learning pathways. There is an understanding that a perfect school does not exist, that conflict is healthy and that making progress consists of making mistakes that are learning opportunities. An inquiry-driven research culture is evident among both student and adult learners. Educators recognise that there can be sloppy mistakes when intentionality is low. However, there are also mistakes that lead to aha moments that can stretch them (Briceño, 2015).

A culture of 'doing' permeates and if harmony exists, individuals are more likely to question the status quo in order to keep evolving rather than becoming complacent and in danger of regressing. They embrace viewpoints that challenge them and accept non-closure and polarities of thinking. Most important, at this stage, the whole school community knows that they can achieve and sustain this work and celebrations of success further motivate the community towards achieving collective goals (Jackson, 2014).

Challenges at this stage can arise if a Totally Inclusive mandate is seen as a passing phase or educational trend instead of a genuine underlying core value for learning and teaching. Competing demands on organizational resources can also threaten to deter from this core work for those who have yet to fully commit to equitable practices. An example of this is schooling during a pandemic. While for some, this may seem to be a competing factor for a school's developmental priority, a school at a Totally Inclusive Stage would ensure that these values are embedded into decision-making at all levels so that the most historically marginalised individuals and groups will continue to have access to learning and teaching. This example shows how Totally Inclusive values are at the heart of an organisation instead of an add-on.

Sustaining an institution at this stage requires a dynamic and cyclical approach to refining one's systems and structures so that continuous evolution into better versions of itself is possible.

Examples of sustaining practices include the following:
- Honest and open feedback mechanisms
- Evaluation protocols to monitor progress and recalibrate for continuous school improvement
- Ensuring that decision-making is research-informed. Research is defined broadly to encompass academic publications, educator experiences and the collection of data ranging from student learning evidence to community perception surveys
- Quality assurance protocols are selected for their embedded DEIJ values. These are chosen to help guide, monitor and evaluate growth
- Deep implementation across systems, structures and policy is evident through consistency of practice, collective efficacy, skill development and continuous reflection (Jacobs and Alcock, 2017)
- Distributive leadership models encourage voice, choice and ownership of learning. Rigid hierarchical leadership structures have been dismantled
- School is authentic and vulnerable about its processes and constant growth
- Maintains a reputation for being a Totally Inclusive School and is able to act as a model for other schools to follow

A Totally Inclusive School continually collects and analyses data and revisits this continuum to ensure that the learning community understands what different stages look like to prevent regression. In short, the institution values monitoring for growth, and documenting and evidencing inclusive practices to help communicate milestones in transparent ways. The school also balances using internal methods to measure growth, with external methods to ensure that assessments are objective. Regular reporting to the school community identifies progress and strengths and celebrates the dynamic learning community in which evolving identities can thrive (Table 9.7).

Table 9.7 Totally Inclusive Stage – Main Characteristics and Examples of Practice

	Continuum descriptors	Practices from the learning community
Behaviours/Mindsets	• School's life and culture reflect full participation and shared power with diverse racial, sexual, gender, cultural and economic groups fully participating and represented equitably. • Members across all identity groups are full participants in decisions that shape the institution and inclusion of diverse cultures, lifestyles, and interests. • A sense of restored trust, community and mutual caring. • Student voices and learner agency continually nurtured to promote Totally Inclusive practices.	**What educators may say** – "How can we use that _____ information to help us adapt to differences?" – "Let's recognize some different perspectives here before deciding on next steps." – "How best can we share what worked for us with others?" – "I wonder how they do _____, let's reach out to help us attend to this challenge." – "Our school stands for _____, and this means that we do/do not _____." – "Let's consider if this practice is meeting all our learners' needs." – "What about _____, how can we be more inclusive?"

[Continued]

163 **The Total Inclusivity Continuum for Schools**

Table 9.7 [Cont.]

Continuum descriptors	Practices from the learning community
Systems/Structures	**Policies and Infrastructure**
• School community works effectively and systematically in ensuring a Totally Inclusive mission, structure, constituency, policies and practices.	DEIJ is central to the school's mission, policies, programmes, decision-making, practice and success.
	Surveys are regularly conducted to monitor progress. Assessment tools and results are used to inform further school planning.
	School board commits, supports, and reports on DEIJ-related initiatives.
• Allies with others in combating all forms of social oppression.	Accountability lies with the head of school and governing body.
• Actively works in larger communities (regional, national, global) to eliminate all forms of oppression and to create intercultural organizations.	DEIJ is a responsibility of all employees and this expectation is communicated clearly. Employees are held accountable for any actions in violation of this expectation.
	Ongoing commitment to professional learning related to DEIJ. This exists in multiple forms (training, coaching, peer observation, professional inquiry groups, etc.) and consists of a wide range of topics to meet individuals' needs.
• School undertakes regular and systemic assessment of strategic actions to evidence growth and ensures all aspects of the school community maintain alignment with these aims.	Recruitment and retention practices systematically ensure that diverse candidates have opportunities and have resulted in a staff constitution that reflects the student and community demographic.
	Demographic metrics are included upon admissions and used to inform learning and teaching design and institutional decision-making.
	School climate ensures the wellbeing and safety of all staff and students. Safeguarding practices are in place and the community has confidence in reporting processes.
	Clear, transparent communication is a norm that transcends traditional hierarchies and power structures.

With a thorough understanding of each stage of the continuum, individuals and institutions are well positioned to self-reflect, identify their stage of development and determine next steps. Keep in mind that transformation takes time. In our final chapter, we explore changing landscapes and what advocacy looks like as we engage every member of the learning community to step up, resist complacency and sustain this ongoing work that should be at the heart of every educator and learner.

CHAPTER NINE: REFLECTION, GUIDANCE AND COMMITMENT

This chapter's reflections come in the form of supplementary materials. Within these, you will find reflection questions that will help guide your exploration, renew your commitment and identification of next steps.

A Road Map for Using the Continuum is a checklist that is organised around three steps.

Step 1   outlines preparations needed before using the continuum.

Step 2   involves exploring the continuum through these driving questions:
- Where is the school currently?
  - o   Identify the behaviours/mindsets and systems/structures found (or lacking) at each stage
- What is the school ready to develop next?
  - o   Initiatives to advocate for to move the school to the next stage

Step 3   moves from talking about perceptions to outlining next steps to put into action. These considerations are starting points, and additional steps relevant to one's school context should be integrated into the process.

A Road Map for Using The Continuum on Becoming a Totally Inclusive School

Step 1: Understand the Continuum and clarify goals
- Identify the motivation of the individual/group using the continuum.
- Consider what are some key goals of the individual/group related to Total Inclusivity.
- Identify who will be using this continuum for reflection and self-assessment.
- Ensure that everyone involved understands all aspects described in the continuum.
  - o Facilitate learning opportunities so that all involved understand the continuum's contents
  - o Complete individual work needed to understand concepts within
- Establish a shared understanding of the purpose of using the contin-uum to identify next steps for school growth, based on individu-al/group perceptions and not as an evaluative tool for teacher or school performance.
- Commit to using this continuum as a reflection tool that is most ef-fective when revisited over time.
- Establish how this tool fits within an overall action plan.
- Allocate resources to facilitate use of this continuum and subsequent follow up actions.
- _____

Step 2: Assess your school using the Continuum on Becoming a Totally Inclusive School
- Use the Continuum Deep Dive template as a starting point for indi-vidual/group use. Modify the tool as needed.
- Facilitate the process of using the continuum as an opportunity for learning and inquiry into Total Inclusivity concepts.
- Embrace the Seven I's of the Totally Inclusive Advocacy Stance.
- _____

Step 3: From talk to walk
- Use the School's Stage and Identifying Initiatives template to help guide the school from talk to walk.
- Create/revise action plans to address:
  o Identification of priority areas for data gathering to substantiate perceptions and establish baseline measurements to track growth.
  o The learning areas revealed, related to behaviours/mindsets, and the resources (time, money, learning opportunities) required to address this factor in need of strengthening.
  o The institutional changes needed, related to systems/structures, including the initiatives to advocate for and implement.
- Reaffirm commitments to Total Inclusivity and determine when the continuum will be reprised
- _____

A Continuum Deep Dive template is designed to support collaborative inquiry. The template can be used to explore any of the six stages. You can use this on your own or with a team. Engaging with each of the six stages is recommended. When considering next steps whilst in the Totally Inclusive stage, it is important to think about what it would take to sustain a school's continuous development so that it remains in this stage. This tool will help you build on the examples that are found within this chapter so that it is relevant for your school's culture and context.

Assessing Your School and Identifying Initiatives template guides reflection through a series of considerations to help prioritise actions to keep, stop or start doing after a specific stage(s) is identified.

CONTINUUM DEEP DIVE TEMPLATE

Supplementary Material 9.2 – Continuum Deep Dive

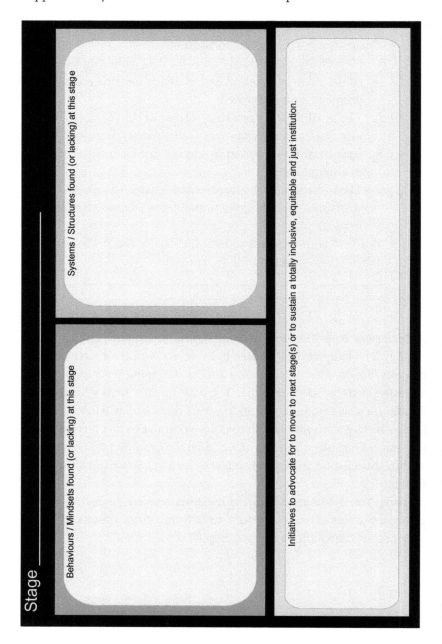

Stage

Systems / Structures found (or lacking) at this stage

Behaviours / Mindsets found (or lacking) at this stage

Initiatives to advocate for to move to next stage(s) or to sustain a totally inclusive, equitable and just institution.

THE SCHOOL'S STAGE AND IDENTIFYING INITIATIVES

1. Current Practice

Which stage of the continuum is your school functioning in? Share key reasons why you have chosen this stage

2. Growth Area Priority

Which specific continuum descriptor or topic related to the identified stage of development garnered the most reflection/debate? Describe why this area should be prioritised.

3. Future Practice

What would be the ideal outcome? Conceptualise and describe the desired state and optimal progress in this area.

Total Inclusivity and Your Institution

4. Areas in Need of Strengthening

Identify the **behaviours/mindsets** in need of strengthening to promote learning and growth in this area.	Identify the **systems/structures** in need of institutional change to address inequities related to this area.

5. Understanding Gaps and Misconceptions

What factors may we be missing that we need to consider or learn more about? What are possible misconceptions, challenges or barriers to learning and development that may arise?

6. Next Steps

Initiative	Timeline/Timeframes	Advocates & Allies	Resources Commitment	Evidence of Progress	Transparency
Action to: • Keep doing (renew), • Stop doing (phase out) • Start doing (new initiative)	Outline the timeline and timeframes. Is this a quick win, short-term, medium–term or long-term action?	Identify the advocates and allies within the school community needed to propel this initiative forward.	Pinpoint the resources commitment required for this initiative to be successful.	Identify how evidence of progress will be documented to monitor and measure success milestones.	Set communication goals to share progress, affirm commitments and address challenges and/or celebrate milestones.

All these supplementary materials are tools to help with the developmental process and to support you with the complexities of becoming a Totally Inclusive School.

REFERENCES

Blackwell, A.G. (2017). The Curb-Cut Effect. *Stanford Social Innovation Review*. www.ssir.org/articles/entry/the_curb_cut_effect#.

Briceño, E. (2015). Why Understanding These Four Types of Mistakes Can Help Us Learn. *KQED*. www.kqed.org/mindshift/42874/why-understanding-these-four-types-of-mistakes-can-help-us-learn.

Cox, E. (1995). *Lecture 2 — Raising Social Capital*. Melbourne: Boyer Lectures.

Hall, E.T. (1976). *Beyond Culture*. New York: Anchor.

Henley, D. (2019). The Importance of Speaking Truth to Power. *Forbes*. www.forbes.com/sites/dedehenley/2019/12/28/the-importance-of-speaking-truth-to-power/?sh=148474b11d32.

IDI Inventory (2020). The Intercultural Development Continuum (IDC). *IDI Inventory*. https://idiinventory.com/generalinformation/the-intercultural-development-continuum-idc/.

Jackson, B. (2014). Chapter 9. Theory and Practice of Multicultural Organization Development. *The NTL Handbook of Organization Development and Change: Principles, Practices, and Perspectives* (pp. 175–192). San Francisco, CA: Wiley.

Jacobs, H. H., & Alcock, M. (2017). *Bold Moves for Schools: How We Create Remarkable Learning Environments*. Alexandria, VA: ASCD.

Kergall, A. (2020). Failure and Success: The Twins of Exponential Self-Growth. *Minute Hack*. www.minutehack.com/opinions/failure-and-success-the-twins-of-exponential-self-growth.

Lindsey, R. B., Robins, K. N., Terrell, R. D., & Lindsey, D. B. (2019). *Cultural Proficiency: A Manual for School Leaders*. Thousand Oaks, CA: Corwin.

Moule, J. (2012). *Cultural Competence: A Primer for Educators*. Belmont, CA: Wadsworth Publishing.

Patel, S. (2021). What "Failing Fast" Really Looks Like: How to Transform Past Failures Into Successes. *Sujanpatel.com*. https://sujanpatel.com/business/failing-fast-2/.

Radd, S. I., Givens, G. Z., Gooden, M. A., & Theoharis, G. (2021). *Five Practices for Equity-focused School Leadership*. Alexandria, VA: ASCD.

Right Question Institute. (2020). What is the Voice in Decisions Technique? *Right Question Institute: A Catalyst for Microdemocracy*. https://rightquestion.org/vidt/.

The Leadership Academy. (2021). School System Equity Self-Assessment. *The Leadership Academy*. www.leadershipacademy.org/resources/school-system-equity-self-assessment/.

Chapter Ten

In January 2021, Amanda Gorman, youth poet laureate of Los Angeles, shared a poem at US president Joe Biden's swearing-in ceremony titled "The Hill We Climb". She wrote the poem shortly after pro-Trump rioters stormed the Capitol Building (Liu, 2021). Gorman recognised that space was needed for grief, horror, hope and unity and used this opportunity to address themes of racial justice, confronting realities and moving forward. Her poem resonated globally as a call to sustain action with courage and hope. To create a Totally Inclusive school that recognises, values, protects and nurtures diverse identities there are 'hills to climb' and we must continually move one foot in front of the other to succeed.

Gorman shared in her poem:

We've learned that quiet isn't always peace
And the norms and notions
of what just is
Isn't always just-ice
And yet the dawn is ours
before we knew it
Somehow we do it

EDUCATIONAL ECOSYSTEM

Educators around the globe, like you, have learned that the education ecosystem as we know it, has widely accepted a normalised structure that 'just is'. To date, students and educators who have been historically marginalised in these systems have felt pressure to assimilate into and comply with this existing structure that privileges a dominant group. Whether the school ecosystem serves all individuals within them or not, "[s]omehow we just do it".

DOI: 10.4324/9781003231233-13

According to *Merriam-Webster's Dictionary* (n.d.), an environmental ecosystem is a complex "community of organisms and its environment functioning as an ecological unit". A school is an ecological unit consisting of complex interdependent parts. In any ecosystem, if there is a lack or an abundance of any one factor this can affect the overall balance and health of the community.

As Slade (2019) wrote in an Association for Supervision and Curriculum Development (ASCD) blog post, "An unsafe environment affects the student's feeling of belonging, her sense of self, his ability to plan long term, her readiness to interact and socialize with others."

Children experiencing oppression in the school system are living with trauma, not free to learn, grow and form their sense of self without challenges and barriers. No child under our care should be in an ecosystem where oppression exists. It is our responsibility as educators to create an educational ecosystem that is a totally inclusive, liberated landscape where all learners have equitable chances to thrive. A learning environment designed to serve the most historically marginalised is one that does not take away from another group. It is a place where learning opportunities are abundant for all and where the barriers experienced by the marginalised are addressed through a school's design, not as an afterthought.

As we have revealed in this book, schools are not just and equitable ecosystems by default. They can only become so through our combined efforts. There are endless possibilities of what schools could be if designed to be places where learners are liberated and have the power to be their authentic selves.

Pushing back against inequitable ecosystems means that one is no longer satisfied with what 'just is' and of being complicit in an inequitable system's upkeep. Educators who are choosing to do nothing are a part of maintaining an inequitable status quo. Each of us co-authors have gone from complicity to advocacy and are continually doing internal work to unlearn cultural norms so that we are able to advocate for the marginalised and the silenced. In some cases, that means speaking up for oneself, and at other times, it is advocating for and supporting others.

Our paths toward advocacy may be personal or professional, or a combination of both. Either way, socially responsible leadership and active citizenship require us to understand ourselves and how we can leverage our privileges and power by taking action. We can say that we care and empathise about issues, but do we really care if we are not turning that emotion into advocacy and action? This is the difference between performative allyship and approaches that hyper-intellectualise diversity, equity, inclusion and justice (DEIJ) work, and true allyship exhibited through one's actions.

TOTAL INCLUSIVITY'S ADVOCACY STANCE

Designing and sustaining a school that serves each and every child is a complex challenge that requires commitment from educators who have advocacy capabilities and are willing to use them. To create a Totally Inclusive school, mindsets that underpin decision-making and positive action need to be cultivated. The Seven I's of Total Inclusivity's Advocacy Stance outlines the key characteristics needed to sustain interventions and initiatives.

An advocate who is an agent of liberation for Total Inclusivity strives to be:

→ **Intentional**
- By engaging with the intention to learn, reflect, grow and take informed actions.

→ **Invitational**
- By including and valuing diverse voices and perspectives through creating spaces that foster psychological safety. Advocates recognise that failures and mistakes are a norm and invite imperfection to drive and accelerate progress.

→ **Inquiry-driven**
- By seeking to understand and construct new understandings. Advocates recognise that Totally Inclusive inquiry involves examining privilege, biases, understanding gaps and diverse ways of knowing.

→ **Interactive**
- By recognising that learning is a social activity that gains meaning through transfer into practice. Advocates value learner agency and aspire to instigate and contribute to initiatives.

→ **Intrepid**
- By facing inequities with fortitude and endurance and recognising that taking courageous actions can require discomfort, risk management and fearlessness.

→ **Impactful**

♦ By considering and aspiring to take actions that result in a Totally Inclusive impact. Advocates also acknowledge and take responsibility for past actions that caused harm, in order to promote healing and growth.

→ **Interconnected**

♦ By recognising that there are multiple entry points and tactics for learning, engagement, advocacy and action. Advocates embrace complexity and acknowledge that dismantling inequities requires interconnected, intersectional approaches at individual and institutional levels.

Adopting the Seven I's of Total Inclusivity, like any skill, takes practice, commitment and clarity about one's goal. Becoming emboldened educators who exemplify an advocacy stance is an approach that builds on the Nine Rs of Reflectivity that were referred to in Chapter One. Whilst the Nine Rs focus on being **reflective**, the Seven I's highlight the importance of being **reflexive**.

Reflection is when individuals learn and develop through examining and considering in-depth reflections **on** actions and reflections **in** actions. This engages individuals and teams in linking theory and practice and considering the why, who, when and what happened. **Reflexivity** requires reflecting in the community to form a wider system (Glanville, 2013). Reflexivity involves being able to identify how one's actions impact a situation. It is more than just reflection, as it demands individuals to determine their positioning in order to understand how our presence, perspectives, biases and behaviours contribute to the construction of the ecosystems that we are a part of (Fook, 2002).

When engaging in reflection and reflexivity, one of the hardest tasks is unlearning white supremacy, recognizing that what we view as professional standards are closely linked with the behaviours and cultural norms we have been conditioned to value over another and that these internalized viewpoints contribute to upholding power disparities (Kim, 2021). For example, to recognise injustices, depending on your identity, you may need to understand the role that paternalism plays; one of the characteristics of white supremacy (Okun, 2021). To recognise paternalism requires an understanding of one's positionality. For example, you may have grown up playing the part of a 'model minority' who defaults to those with decision-making power and think that their problem-solving strategy is taken in the best interest of all (Kim, 2021).

The normalisation of dominant culture conditions is reflected in mindsets and behaviours that do not serve all of us. It is in our conditioning to interpret the cultures and systems we are a part of as 'norms' and to assign value to them. Challenging these norms requires us to think critically and make emotional investments. To be both reflective and reflexive, we need to consider our own position and choices.

For change to take hold, we need to continue learning and reflecting, and think reflexively about how we can change systems and structures. Change cannot happen if we are only looking back. We need to use our knowledge, and the information that we have and can gather, to inform our next steps.

As Barack Obama (2008) said in a speech to supporters in Chicago, US: "Change will not come if we wait for some other person or if we wait for some other time. We are the ones we've been waiting for. We are the change that we seek."

Meaningful change occurs when individuals or groups use their voice to question common practice to bring about greater equity (Aow, 2021). So let's initiate change with intention.

But how will we know what we need to change from? Establishing a shared understanding of the key issues and gathering and leveraging data to not only identify the problems that exist but also inspire and initiate meaningful change is essential. The following section outlines possible pathways to take to help you learn more about your current landscape and pinpoint the next steps to focus on for both individual and institutional growth.

IDENTIFYING YOUR SCHOOL'S CURRENT LANDSCAPE

The previous chapter touched on two possible entry points for using the Total Inclusivity Continuum for schools, starting with data collection to help determine your school's stage of development or reflecting on the continuum first and then identifying areas for data collection. Both pathways serve the same purpose – to gain insights into the learning landscape of your school context and culture so that you can make informed choices aimed at having a lasting impact. Identification of the "what" helps us leverage positive forces and develop interventions to mitigate challenges.

Some would argue that it is essential to establish baseline measures so that growth can be measured, tracked and reported on. This paragraph may resonate with your own beliefs about the use of data in school improvement. Testing to measure progress and drive better results was supposed to fix the education system, and unsurprisingly, it has not (Rodberg, 2019). 'Traditional' tools used to grade, research and assess based on evaluative criteria, comparable models and classification and categorization of data are deeply embedded in Western ways of knowing. Safir and Dugan (2021) offer us an alternative, pushing us to reimagine how data can be humanizing, liberatory and healing. They write that "[i]t's time to repurpose data from a tool for accountability and oppression to a tool for learning and transformation" and that "street data will help us pivot from blind compliance with external mandates to cultivating local, human-centered, critical judgment" (Safir & Dugan, 2021, p. 53).

For our purposes, the term *data* is broadly defined to include voices, stories, observations and experiences. We must then consider how this information can be used to co-construct a liberated landscape in our school. Multiple forms of data can provide anchor points to inform decision-making, but tools such as surveys and rubrics have been historically valued more than stories and accounts of lived experiences. This over-reliance on quantifiable data has fed a narrative that emphasises directional indicators instead of the behaviours needed to achieve them (Hurt, 2021). 'Types of Street Data' help us identify root causes and hunches that we can act on (Safir & Dugan, 2021, p. 62). Educators on the ground, walking the same spaces as the students they impact, know that what is widely measurable is not the same as what is valuable (Safir & Dugan, 2021). What is valuable is not the data that is gathered just for the sake of proving that something exists. Data proves its worth if it is able to move individuals into action.

TOOLS TO HELP GAIN INSIGHTS ABOUT YOUR LEARNING LANDSCAPE

Choosing the right data collection tool for you or your school will depend on your intent. Some tools are focused on individual mindsets and behaviours, others on organisational systems and structures and some address both. The process of choosing a tool is an inquiry process that should be driven by you and your school's values. This process should also reflect your needs. Tools to help you gain insights about your learning landscape have been included in this chapter.

When educators design a unit of work, they identify the learning outcome so they can be intentional about learning and teaching goals. Educators also consider how success will be measured and select the learning tools that will support students to achieve these goals. The same process and principles apply to choosing a suitable tool to help you understand your school's landscape. What is your intended outcome? How will you know you've reached it?

To begin with, we have to consider the diversity that exists within our communities. Over time, a school's demographics change. Depending on your school's mission and related admissions policy, you may feel that your community is very diverse, 'monocultural' or something in between. In our opinion, every community is diverse. Beyond what one may perceive on the surface, there is always a diversity of perspectives, religious and cultural views, lifestyles, beliefs about schooling and more in every community. Therefore, it is important to regularly identify a school community's demographics to have a chance to gain insights and further understand how best to serve them.

To choose the most suitable survey tool different factors should be taken into consideration. For example, is the school looking to survey the community to determine factual information about the diversity present in their community, or are they seeking community members' perceptions on their sense of belonging? Whatever the purpose, Table 10.1 offers some considerations.

Taking these considerations into account, one should also be aware of the possible implications of using a survey tool as an audit of just another initiative. As Huang (2021) shares, a common misstep is when schools engage in performative "Doing Equity" work (Safir & Dugan, 2021). Huang (2021) writes that surface-level DEIJ work looks like "when equity and justice work is treated as a series of tools, strategies, and compliance tasks versus a whole person, whole systems change processes linked to identity, history, culture, and healing".

By considering how survey tools can be used (i.e. to learn more about perceptions from different community members in a school), we hope that schools will shift away from looking at these as audit tools. Instead, they should see these perception surveys as opportunities to gain new knowledge and perspectives in order to make informed decisions.

Table 10.1 Considerations When Surveying Your Landscape

Move away from ...	Move towards ...
Choosing a survey tool to check off a DEIJ initiative box and sharing the results to show how diverse the school is. An act like this is performative and weaponizes the information for branding purposes only.	Clarifying the purpose of using a survey tool and ensuring that the purpose is linked to specific DEIJ related initiatives. Clarity includes defining how the final results will be used.
Making assumptions about how people identify themselves and using long-established systems that may not have been designed inclusively. E.g. Will the survey make assumptions about individuals' identity markers?	Researching current industry practices and modifying data collection tools to reflect inclusive terminology. E.g. Broadening understanding of the diversity of gender identities and including these in survey choices.
Leadership group deciding on what to survey behind closed doors and then implementing their plan. Top-down decision making like this can lead to community confusion about what the purpose of the survey is.	Setting up discussions with members of target groups to identify key issues. Involving a cross-section of representatives from the school community helps build understanding, increase transparency and provides a range of perspectives.
Choosing a survey and running it without piloting or re-adjusting the questionnaire.	Testing the survey with a pilot group to identify adjustments needed.
Selecting respondents to influence survey results (consciously or unconsciously).	Ensuring that the respondents and data collection method allows valid conclusions to be drawn.
Analysing results and making conclusions that the information gained are facts.	Interpreting results as perceptions and taking into account response rates and the way respondents were selected.
Deciding on a new initiative based on results without sharing the process of how this was reached.	Sharing survey results and conclusions in conjunction with how results were reached. Clarify connections between survey results and identification of next step initiatives.

Components adapted from the OECD's (2012) Measuring Regulatory Performance: A Practitioner's Guide to Perception Surveys.

Total Inclusivity and Your Institution

The following are some options that educational organisations have found useful as they began to inquire into which tool would be most suitable for their own school context. As you consider these options, be sure to keep in mind the overall purpose of using such a tool and how the information will be used to inform next-step initiatives.

SAMPLE TOOLS

The Intercultural Development Inventory

The Intercultural Development Inventory (IDI) helps individuals or groups understand the challenges they may face in achieving their goals. Knowing one's orientation and the next steps one could take to move along this developmental continuum will help individuals and groups achieve more effective actions for social justice. For example, if one has an orientation in the earlier stages of the continuum (Denial or Polarization), then one is likely to be in need of ways to manage their unconscious biases. Administrators of the IDI can debrief individuals who also receive an Individual Development Plan (IDP; Hammer, 2012/2021). The IDP can be completed independently or in conjunction with further consultation with a Qualified Administrator.

The advantage of this tool is that the results provide individuals with a Perceived Orientation and a Developmental Orientation. People often overestimate their level of intercultural competence and the orientation gap between one's perception and developmental orientation has the potential to bring forth a greater understanding of how one may think they behave with good intentions but may not always be having the intended impact. To have comparable data, the IDI would need to be re-administered. A disadvantage of using this tool is that the quality of one's experience with the IDI will depend on the qualified administrator consultant and their ability to address individual and/or institutional needs. A poorly administered IDI may lead to misunderstandings, confusion and a possible widening of polarized mindsets. More information about the tool can be found on the IDI website.

The IDI is accessible across cultures, and it is available in 17 different languages. This option bears costs dependent on the administrator consultant used.

Follow this QR code to the IDI website:
https://idiinventory.com

Survey Tool for Teachers

The inquiry *Self-survey* for teachers and the inquiry *Student-survey* by Mitchell (2019), found in her book *Experience Inquiry: 5 powerful strategies, 50 practical experiences*, offers a practical and easy-to-administer tool for self-reflection and analysis. Both surveys consist of 10 questions and ask one to rate on a scale ranging from 0 = *absolutely not true* [yet] to 10 = *unequivocally true* (Mitchell, n.d.). Statements in the teacher's Self-survey ask for reflections about the strength of relationships with students and whether there is equal verbal participation between students in one's classroom. This stimulates thinking about voices in the classroom, relationships and teacher preferences towards adopting an invitational teaching stance.

In the *Student-survey*, it asks for reflections on statements about how well your teacher knows you, if the teacher asks a lot of really good questions and if students get to make many choices in class. Some statements between the two surveys are directly related so that an educator can compare their own self-perception with those of their students. Understanding if characteristics of an advocacy stance are present in the classroom will assist teachers with identifying personal goals to enhance their learning and teaching approaches.

The Inquiry surveys are also accessible across and only entail the cost of a book to add to your professional library.

Follow this QR code to the Inquiry Partners website: https://www.inquirypartners.com/resources

A survey service that may suit your culture and context is the American-based YouthTruth Student Survey non-profit that offers schools and districts student, family and staff surveys with questions that include core themes such as relationships, belonging and peer collaboration, school culture, obstacles to learning and optional customized topics related to diversity, equity and inclusion and student voice and leadership (YouthTruth Student Survey: A National Non-profit, 2021).

Youth Truth Student Survey website. https://youthtruthsurvey.org/

Total Inclusivity and Your Institution

Global Equality Collective App

The mission of the Global Equality Collective (GEC) is to support educators in becoming diversity and inclusion experts in their own contexts. This tool aims to simplify the process of working towards equality, diversity and inclusion with two simple checkbox assessments, one for the leadership team and another for staff. They survey across 11 different areas ranging from inclusion and belonging, leadership and values, culture, working life and policies to sexism and sexual harassment and more.

To administer the GEC app, the school completes a self-assessment survey and the employee-assessment survey, composed of partner questions, before launching it across the community. This gives schools a complete 360-degree view of their equality and inclusion status helping to pinpoint gaps and areas for further development. This app is uniquely affordable and with a membership to the collective one gains access to a training platform that is built for educators. The app was developed over 3 years of evidence-based academic research by experts and leading UK universities (GEC, n.d.). This dynamic tool promises to make DEIJ advocacy accessible to as many educators as possible through its easy-to-use interface and multiple learning pathways.

Follow this QR code to the GEC app website:
https://thegec.org/theapped

Culture Amp Survey Tool

Culture Amp (n.d.) aims to "help facilitate a grassroots, bottom-up movement of HR professionals and people leaders committed to improving the employee experience across their organizations". Schools are in the people business, and we can learn a great deal from organizations that don't just crunch numbers but are also committed to connecting the dots to elevate engagement, development, performance and retention (Culture Amp, n.d.). Culture Amp provides a DEI Starter Kit after you create a free account. The platform is intuitive and allows you to prepare and customise a diversity and inclusion survey for your workplace. Like the GEC App, Culture Amp's services aim to have institutions choose the learning and development pathways that best suit one's culture and context.

Follow this QR code to the Culture Amp website: https://www.cultureamp.com/

The Uhlala PRIDE Index

This audit is free of charge, and one can compare their results with 30 companies listed on the Deutscher Aktien Index (DAX), the German Stock Exchange. The questionnaire is available in German and English for large organizations of 500 or more employees and for small to medium-sized organizations of up to 500 employees (UHLALA Group, n.d.). A student support services coordinator working in an international school in Hong Kong completed the 30- to 60-minute, online PRIDE Index audit and found it a useful tool to expand beyond their own thinking about considerations their school should take to make their institution more inclusive for LGBT+ people. At present, there is no charge to create an account and gain access to the index questionnaire, and one can even share it with others within one's institution.

Follow this QR code to the UHLALA website: https://uhlala.com/en/how-lgbt-friendly-are-you-as-an-employer/

Over time, new tools will become available, and others will become outdated. What is important is inquiring into what is currently available, choosing a tool that will fit your purpose and moving forward with clarity of intention.

DESIGNING YOUR OWN SURVEY

Here are six steps to keep in mind when designing a survey from the OECD (2012) guide to *Measuring Regulatory Performance: A Practitioner's Guide to Perception Surveys*:

1. Define survey objectives, use of results and target population
2. Draft survey questions
3. Pilot and re-adjust the questionnaire
4. Select respondents and the data collection method
5. Run the survey
6. Analyse the results

Unpacking each step is important before launching into creating a survey of one's own. Since a self-created tool is not externally validated, pilot and readjustment stages are vital to test and check that the survey will serve one's defined objectives before launch. When selecting who to send the survey to, it is important to determine how respondents are selected (random or other) and that the sampling size allows conclusions to be drawn from the results. Data collection method options include personal interviews, telephone interviews, internet surveys and email surveys and should be chosen to maximise one's response rate as well as the quality of responses. The analysis of results is crucial and where next-step interventions can be identified. It is important when analysing results to take into consideration that any interpretations of results are perceptions rather than facts. Also that these aspects need to be taken into consideration during the analysis: the response rate, number of respondents and selection method.

STORIES THAT MOVE

Sharing stories humanises this important work. Educators' experiences and stories of how the school ecosystem impacts individuals have been historically undervalued compared to quantitative or qualitative data measured using formal tools such as inventories, surveys, rubrics or continuums. While these formalised methods can help create a baseline from which to measure growth, it is the stories our school community tells that truly show us the impact our school design has on the humans within it.

Garmston (2018) stresses that 'data does not move people. Stories do'. Garmston explains how hearing a story can arouse empathy and cooperation and promote behaviours intended to help others. When stories are used to persuade, they can be more effective than data, reports, studies or PowerPoint presentations (Garmston, 2018). Storytelling can serve different functions such as shifting perceptions, inviting learning, inspiring action and leading others to the liberated landscape of a Totally Inclusive school. Stories can stem from life experiences, work experiences, school experiences, cultural heritage and more. They may be shared in planned or unplanned spaces and may enlighten problematic behaviours, be they stories of inspirational advocacy or simply told as a means of seeking affinity and connections with others. Given that stories are one of the most powerful forms of data that individuals share, it is important to strategise how we enrich storytelling.

Cultivating safe spaces where stories can be shared can look like the following scenarios: book clubs and discussions, forums hosted by students, guest speakers with question-and-answer (Q&A) sessions, blogs, podcasts, starting meetings with story sharing and more. Each learning community will determine what is most appropriate for their school's culture and context. Depending on the school's existing ecosystem, the notion of a courageous storytelling space will look different. In one school, speaking up at a meeting with a contradictory opinion takes an intrepid educator; in another, this may be the norm if diverse perspectives are encouraged. Whatever climate you find yourself in, the power of stories to persuade and invite reflection is worth the commitment. Push for the creation of safe, interactive spaces, because the potential reward is the catalyst for learning, prompt action and improvements to difficult situations (Garmston, 2018).

To assist in facilitating conversations, Singleton (2006/2014) advises the following:

- Expect to Experience Discomfort
- Stay Engaged
- Speak Your Truth
- Expect and Accept a Lack of Closure

These four approaches provide protocols to help foster the cultivation of safe spaces where communities can explore and negotiate understandings of complex issues. Getting comfortable with discomfort is not easy, as people are often conditioned to 'keep the peace', 'to go along to get along' or, as some school community members have shared, "I was brought up not to talk about race/sexuality/money." Creating these spaces relies on people within a community to reframe their fear of these topics, be vulnerable, and, as a consequence, build relationships and trust. This requires embracing awkwardness, cutting people some slack, speaking up and sharing the impact; however, it may make people feel (Neville, 2019). In essence, one needs to fully embrace a Totally Inclusive advocacy stance in order to develop the skills necessary to have courageous conversations.

In Chapter Six, a common misstep was shared where the desire to cultivate safe spaces instead led to a tokenistic event that centred the gaze of white people, instead of the Black, Indigenous and People of Colour (BIPOC) guest speakers. To avoid this misstep, it is important to decenter the needs of the privileged. This begins with shifting resources to where they are needed and redistributing power so that the most marginalised needs are met (Kim, 2021). What 'just is' has been created under a white gaze, where whiteness and the privileges that come with it are the default and decisions about how stories are told are filtered through these lenses. The same can be said for a patriarchal gaze, colonial gaze, heteronormative gaze and others. The historically marginalised must not be burdened to share stories so that privileged individuals have learning experiences. Burdening these individuals only presents another opportunity for possible trauma.

This brings us back to the importance of having clarity of purpose. What is the purpose of the storytelling or cultivation of space where stories can be shared? What is the intended outcome? How will these data be accessed and leveraged to elevate advocacy for and actioning of DEIJ-related initiatives? The answer to these questions lies within your learning community. The design and processes used to cultivate these storytelling spaces require an invitational stance. An approach that calls for the inclusion and valuing of diverse voices and perspectives, and the recognition that failures and mistakes are a norm as one paves paths to drive progress (not perfection). Table 10.2 offers some considerations to take.

Student voices and alumni who have experienced the school ecosystems are key voices that schools need to prioritise listening to. They are the reason why we are educators. Stories that Move (2016), a social movement in collaboration with the Anne Frank Museum, offer youth stories from across Europe that were cultivated through anti-discrimination projects. The educators working within this project highlight the importance of listening, dialoguing and showing sensitivity to the vulnerability of the learners under their care when discussing different forms of discrimination at an analytical level (Stories that Move, 2016).

Whether one is cultivating stories from within the school community or sharing stories that help enlighten DEIJ issues from external resources, what is most important is that we do not linger in an existing state where stories persistently tell the same tales of racism,

Table 10.2 Considerations for Cultivating Stories

Move away from ...	Move towards ...
Hosting a one-off, stand-alone event that asks historically marginalised people to share their stories of pain and trauma. This centres the needs of the privileged and shifts the burden of emotional and educational labour onto the marginalised (Kim, 2021).	Decentring the needs of the privileged. Offering alternate ways to access stories or case studies that illuminate DEIJ issues. E.g. Arts & literature, videos, anti-discrimination resources, etc.
Making assumptions about the stories that will be shared and establishing parameters to try and control the outcome.	Creating flexible storytelling spaces and supporting truth telling with open, invitational, inquiry.
Leadership deciding on the stories to be collected and shared to meet hidden agendas.	Involving a cross-section of representations from the school community to organise, tell, share and synthesise data arising from stories.
Silencing stories that challenge the status quo (consciously or unconsciously). E.g. by gaslighting, gatekeeping or engaging in retaliatory behaviour in response to stories that challenge a listener with power and positionality.	Ensuring that storytellers are believed, listened to with open-mindedness and safeguarded.
Interpreting stories as solitary incidents that are not interconnected to the school's ecosystem and treating them as exceptions rather than valid data.	Acknowledging that stories told are reflections of and results of the impact of the school's ecosystem. Issues enlightened by these stories provide data to help identification of next step initiatives.

sexism, classism or any other form of discrimination without intentionally focusing on what our desired state is and how we can leverage the resources we have to reach it (Garmston, 2018).

IDENTIFYING INITIATIVES THROUGH DATA

All the data schools hold are information. If this information is synthesised and analysed, connections can be made to make us more knowledgeable. It is important to gather data to inform us about existing inequities and to track progress over time. When designing for Total Inclusivity, we need data with action potential. For example, a school collects the linguistic profiles of students and families on admission to the school. In addition to this, faculty and support staff linguistic profile data are also collected. With this knowledge, a school is able to gain insight into how to allocate their resources to support home languages and strive towards greater representation of languages (and cultures) in their purchasing of educational materials.

Educators make decisions at any point in time based on what they know. These decisions often involve making connections between multiple sources of data, information and knowledge. For example, a teacher receives a new student in their class who speaks Japanese and has limited skills in the language of instruction of the school (English). The teacher has been working with her homeroom class to develop identity profiles and has learned that two students in class have commonalities with the new student. One student is Japanese and speaks the language at home. Another student who was born in Japan, speaks the language, is a citizen of the host country and recently transitioned to the school after their family repatriated. The teacher is able to use their insights and wisdom to move beyond a surface-level choice of pairing Japanese students together to finding a buddy with recent experience and the requisite skills to help break down possible transition barriers.

This is one specific example of a teacher making one decision to support a learner under their care. It has been postulated that teachers make on average 1,500 decisions daily. These decisions are influenced by a complex combination of factors, many of which have been described in this book. These decisions may be influenced by our unconscious biases and are certainly driven by our underlying core beliefs and values. To help focus educators on designing for equity and keeping total inclusivity at the forefront of thinking, here are three guiding questions:

- How can learner diversity, experiences and perspectives enhance the learning process?
- How do different ways of knowing impact a learner's understanding, skill development and transference of learning?
- How can assessments be differentiated to meet the needs of diverse learners?

With these questions in mind, a teacher can facilitate learning and contribute to the development of the human beings under their care. However, none of these questions can successfully be sustained if a whole school's culture is not underpinned by the same values, we have advocated for throughout this book. Our learners exist in a whole community, not just within individual teachers' classrooms.

CULTURE AND STRATEGY

A famous saying attributed to management consultant Peter Drucker is that "culture eats strategy for breakfast" (Engel, 2018). Instead of looking at these as two constructs in opposition to each other, consider that both culture **and** strategy are polarities to be leveraged. Without a strategy, culture cannot be leveraged, and without a strong culture, one's strategy will not be successful.

Consider the data you may have or plan to collect. What does it tell you about your school's culture? School culture includes the written and unwritten rules that inform educators about how the school functions. This encompasses the institutional history, cultural norms and an understanding of what constitutes acceptable behaviour. The culture shows us how the school collectively values diversity as a fact, right and resource. This is revealed through how community members treat each other with respect and dignity. A positive learning culture in a school that is safe, secure and thriving exhibits these elements:

- Personal and collective well-being – psychological, physical, spiritual safety
- Learner agency and collaboration – all community members are seen as learners and there is collective action-taking and accountability for actions (and inactions)
- Voices in decision-making – shared leadership, choice and ownership of learning

The extent to which a school can lead change interventions depends on both the mindsets of individuals and the conditions for change. We are not going to make progress if we do not understand the way people behave and why. These conduits for change are cultivated through the implementation of policies within the school's ecosystem. Therefore, a part of why we teachers do what we do is both culture **and** strategy. Strategy is more than an action plan consisting of to-do list items. Our policies, systems, and structures are all devices our strategy has put in place. When identifying initiatives to develop, we need to design our next steps in service of the historically marginalised identities within our communities. This aspiration will subsequently serve all identities through a curb-cut effect.

Like any other school initiative, navigating change management is vital, and advocacy towards Total Inclusivity will consist of the shifts and challenges associated with achieving transformation. To implement successful interventions and initiatives, multiple components need to be in place (Tables 10.3 and 10.4).

IDENTIFYING NEXT STEPS

There will be many areas that one can prioritise, and a common question is, "Where do I start?" Engaging with the Continuum on Becoming a Totally Inclusive School presented in Chapter Nine will help you consider the areas where work may be needed and to pinpoint areas that require your immediate focus. Data collection for specific purposes will help you plan and implement effective initiatives. The *Change Components Model* helps with identifying six aspects of whole school development that requires attention in order to progress towards Total Inclusivity. These components are closely interconnected, and multiple components may be in need of attention at the same time.

Table 10.3 The *Total Inclusivity Change Components Model* offers a broad view of the key components needed to navigate and implement change

Aspirational Vision of Total Inclusivity	Commitment	Mindsets & Skills	Agency	Resources	Strategy & Action Plan	=	Success
Aspirational Vision of Total Inclusivity		Mindsets & Skills	Agency	Resources	Strategy & Action Plan	=	**Confusion**
Aspirational Vision of Total Inclusivity	Commitment		Agency	Resources	Strategy & Action Plan	=	**Competition**
Aspirational Vision of Total Inclusivity	Commitment	Mindsets & Skills		Resources	Strategy & Action Plan	=	**Anxiety**
Aspirational Vision of Total Inclusivity	Commitment	Mindsets & Skills	Agency		Strategy & Action Plan	=	**Disengagement**
Aspirational Vision of Total Inclusivity	Commitment	Mindsets & Skills	Agency	Resources	Strategy & Action Plan	=	**Frustration**
Aspirational Vision of Total Inclusivity	Commitment	Mindsets & Skills	Agency	Resources		=	**False Starts & Stagnation**

Adapted from Knoster, T., Villa, R., Thousand, J. (2000). A framework for thinking about systems change. In R. Villa and J. Thousands (Eds.) *Restructuring for caring and effective education: Piecing the puzzle together* (2nd edition). Baltimore: Paul H. Brookes. With reference to: Powell, W. & Kusuma-Powell, O. (2013). *NFI Inclusive Toolkit* (p. 113) Next Frontier Inclusion.

Table 10.4 *What Happens When a Component Is Missing: The Consequences Explained* details the possible pitfalls that impede progress when one of these key components is not attended to

All components present	Success	A school ecosystem with DEIJ values. Every individual feels a sense of belonging. Diversity is seen as a fact, right and resource and school design are underpinned by aspirations to create equitable access to learning. School improves continuously. DEIJ values prevail.
Missing: Aspirational Vision of Total Inclusivity	**Confusion**	Lack of clarity about the school's aspirational DEIJ-related goals. Vision of inclusion is not widely understood, and pockets of advocacy may exist but be viewed as isolated bandwagons. Absence of a common language and understanding leads to misunderstanding and regress. Confusion prevails as there isn't an aspirational vision to guide decision-making.
Missing: Commitment	**Competition**	The absence of commitment from governance and leadership leads to open and covert sabotage behaviours as consensus, resources and sponsorship is lacking. This lack of sponsorship can empower educators to be non-committal to DEIJ values and initiatives. Focus on DEIJ is seen as a low priority and in competition with other learning and teaching initiatives. Without buy-in from community members across the school ecosystem, change initiatives may be hampered by subversive, competitive behaviours. Lack of accountability prevails.
Missing: Mindsets & Skills	**Anxiety**	Individual beliefs and values of all stakeholders are not yet aligned to Total Inclusivity values and aspirations. Limited intercultural competence skills. Absence of supportive mindsets leads to distrust and sense of hopelessness for sustainable change. Collectively, the community is still developing the necessary skills to effect change, and anxiety is prevalent across the community. Anxiety about failing prevails.

Missing: Agency	**Disengagement**	Without learner agency, individuals lack self-driven engagement and may be unmotivated to take intentional actions. Intrinsic motivation for this work is needed as DEIJ advocacy is emotionally demanding and complex. Without voice, choice and ownership initiatives can be hampered by passivity, division or resistance. People stick to continue doing what is comfortable (the old way).
Missing: Resources	**Frustration**	Without sufficient human and material resources, educators are unable to further develop the competencies and skills necessary to do this work. Without a chance to upskill to make sustainable progress, educators end up feeling frustrated. The most sought-after resource in a school, time, is not given to engage with DEIJ initiatives. Resources such as books, materials and access to professional development are not prioritised. Frustration prevails.
Missing Strategy & Action Plan	**False Starts & Stagnation**	Commitment and enthusiasm are present. There are a lot of meetings, talk and resources and support are available. However, when strategies are not identified and a whole school action plan is lacking there will be a lot of efforts but not a lot of progress being made, resembling a 'treadmill'. There is an increased amount of 'false starts' as change processes are started, but steps and stages are missed. This slows down the process and possibly creates regress. Without a strategy that encompasses data to monitor and evaluate success or regress, the school is less able to identify and share milestones or challenges and modify next step actions. Without strategy and implementation of an action plan criticism, cynicism, negativity and complacency prevail.

LEARNING STORIES: CASES AND REFLECTION QUESTIONS

The following cases have been collected from educators across the globe. They have been anonymised and are offered as scenarios for you to consider and put what you have learned throughout this book into practice. Some of these learning stories may resonate with you more than others. You are likely to have your own learning story. The questions following each story will help spark your own reflection, questioning and reflexive action taking.

Learning Story 1

In a K–12 school with 1500 students and 200 faculty and support staff, a secondary school educator was appointed as the school's part-time DEIJ coach. They led and coached a committee of 22 educators, a student committee (20+ people) and section subcommittees (e.g. primary school educators) on a variety of DEIJ-related initiatives. Initiatives included running parent information workshops, promoting equitable hiring practices, gathering resources and offering training for the board, developing student-led surveys and integrating lessons in homeroom classes and more. Committees met before and after school. They were supported and celebrated by leadership when initiatives aligned with school-wide plans.

The DEIJ committee had an aspirational vision; however, consensus and commitment were not present from the leadership team and school board. While committee members were further developing their mindsets and skills, their resources were limited to widen their outreach to others in the community. Their initiatives were not prioritised in school-wide meeting schedules. The committee had prepared information and training for the governing body but struggled to be put onto the agenda.

Political and increased media narratives about equality and justice raised parent concerns about the DEIJ work done in the school. Five per cent of parents signed a petition against the DEIJ coach and pushed back against the equity work taking place in the school. The school board reacted by publishing a statement that all DEIJ work will be paused as the school re-evaluates the work of the committee within the culture and context of the school. The DEIJ committee was not consulted and felt that their work over the last 3 to 4 years was devalued.

- What stage of development do you think the school was at on the Continuum on Becoming a Totally Inclusive School and why?
- What were positive conduits available in the school community that fostered growth?
- What were the negative forces that impeded change?
- How did a lack of consensus and commitment sabotage DEIJ efforts?
- What interventions need to happen in order for the school not to regress?

Learning Story 2

A qualified, experienced, Black female teacher candidate from Lesotho is interviewing for a primary school teaching position in Western Europe. Their resume shows that they have a master's in educational leadership but not so many years of teaching experience. The candidate also shared that she and her husband moved here after he was offered a position in a biomedical company, and they got married recently. After the interview the principal, who interviewed the candidate, shared with the deputy principal that

- they were impressed by her English skills,
- they didn't like how she bragged about her accomplishments,
- they had concerns that the candidate may start a family soon, and
- thought that the other candidate may be a better fit.

The deputy principal was uncomfortable with the conversation and wanted to follow up but was unsure of what to do next.

REFLECTION QUESTIONS

- What biases were at play in this scenario?
- How did microaggressive behaviour hamper this candidate's chances of landing this role?
- What assumptions can be inferred from this scenario?

- If you were the deputy principal, how would you approach a follow-up conversation with the principal?
- What systems and structures related to hiring practices are in need of strengthening?

Learning Story 3

A high school has been in the news lately as alumni formed a #BlackatSchool Instagram page and regularly share stories from students who experienced racism at the school. This was picked up by a local news outlet, and the school received bad press. Students currently attending the school were empowered by the actions of Alumni to form a #BlackLivesMatter group and had meetings with interested students. The student group is planning on hosting a courageous conversation circle to discuss the anonymous alumni stories. They approached a math teacher that they trust and asked if they could use their classroom space to host the after-school event.

The school hosted training sessions when the news first broke out related to unconscious bias and culturally responsive pedagogy. These took place on staff development days, but teachers have not heard about any antiracism- or DEIJ-related initiatives for more than 3 months. The math teacher is unsure what to do next. Whilst the school has made efforts to support growth in this area to address issues, the math teacher is in their second year of teaching at the school and is wary of making waves as their contract is up for renewal.

REFLECTION QUESTIONS
- What mindsets/behaviours are present in this scenario?
- How can this new initiative and student voices be supported?
- What were positive conduits available in the school community that fostered growth?
- What were the negative forces that impeded change?
- Which change model component(s) is in need of attention?
- What next steps could the math teacher take?

Learning Story 4

A curriculum coordinator living in Germany was on maternity leave and found out after returning to work, and negotiating a new part-time role, that she had regressed on the pay scale. She discovered that despite remaining an employee throughout a 15-month maternity leave period, she had spent an entire financial year off the payroll and as a result did not progress on the yearly pay-scale rise. The coordinator saw a systemic injustice in this and realised that what may seem like a small hiccup in one's earnings would have a large long-term impact on her overall wage earnings and contribution to her pension fund. Realising that on average across the Organisation for Economic Co-operation and Development (OECD) countries 70% of teachers are women (OECD/UIS/Eurostat, 2020), she felt compelled to voice her concerns.

When the coordinator brought this up to the head of school, instead of correcting this injustice, it was turned into a (white) man's personal learning experience about how the pay system worked (or, in this case, did not work). This event and a career spent observing the barriers that women in education face (and the bigger problem of the lack of career obstacles for men, regardless of performance) sparked an interest in the coordinator in all things related to gender inequity in education (Chamorro-Premuzic, 2013). The drive to advocate for self and others led the author to establish a grassroots #WomenEd affinity group in Germany in support of women in education.

REFLECTION QUESTIONS
- What systems/structures are present (or missing) in this scenario? Do you have suggestions for how these could be strengthened?
- What role did paternalism and privilege play?
- Which characteristics of Total Inclusivity's Advocacy Stance were evident in the coordinator?
- What interventions need to happen in order for the school to become more equitable?

Learning Story 5

A school has engaged a group of DEIJ advocates in training, and as a result of this, educators across the institution have spear-headed new initiatives, DEIJ positions have been appointed and time has been allocated to address issues across different school teams. Most of the initiatives relate to gender diversity and LGBTQ+ advocacy. Initiatives include changing a school's uniform policy, redesigning bathroom spaces to be inclusive of gender diversity, LGBTQ-related engagements across PRIDE month and student-led LGBTQ+ affinity and advocacy groups. Overall feelings of progress, raised consciousness and actions have made members of the school community who identify as LGBTQ+ feel a greater sense of belonging. This was evident in conversation circles and a perception survey that was readministered recently.

In addition to this progress, there have been discussions in the DEIJ committee that very little movement has happened on the anti-racism front. The school made a statement in the summer of 2020 about having an anti-bias, anti-racism stance. However, since then, any initiatives suggested by the school's DEIJ advocates related to race have not received the same sponsorship as LGBTQ+ initiatives. The committee discussed how there is a strong perception that it's easier for the school to talk about gender and LGBTQ+ than it is to talk about race and are regrouping to develop their next-step strategy.

REFLECTION QUESTIONS

- What stage of development do you think the school was at on the Becoming a Totally Inclusive School Continuum, and what makes you say that?
- What next steps would you suggest so that the school continues to foster growth?
- What interventions need to happen in order for the school not to regress?
- Which change model component(s) is in need of attention?

As you connect with these learning stories and think about your own practice, there is one persistent barrier to highlight. This is the narrative that "[p]arents do not want their child learning about (insert identity trait here)" or that "We can't do that as we have to answer to parents who are on the board/pay taxes/pay our wages/are our 'clients'." These arguments may also be commonly used when a school's beliefs about curriculum, pedagogy and assessment conflict with a parents' beliefs and values (and memory) about what successful learning looks like. Responses to such challenges tend to be to educate parents about the school's philosophies and practices rather than conceding. It is imperative that we do the same to address the perceived parent barrier to Total Inclusivity and move forward by identifying interventions to mitigate this gap rather than using it as an excuse for inaction or regression. Lumping all 'parents' into one category is also failing to see the diversity within our parent community. Building alliances and leveraging a community's support will be integral to your initiative's success. Put simply, making decisions based on assumptions about what parents want doesn't work. Research shows that the number one distraction from achieving one's mission in schools is appeasing the parents (Hattie, 2015). Schools that are looking to gain momentum and make progress must understand the need to involve parents to build understanding and partnerships for learning. At times, this may require taking an intrepid stance, at the risk of losing enrolment and those colleagues whose beliefs may not align with the school's commitments to Total Inclusivity. On the flip side, your school will be building a reputation as one with strong moral values and ethical leadership, and this will attract families and educators whose beliefs align with your school's vision.

CALL TO ACTION

All journeys begin with putting one foot in front of the other; even walking is a skill we had to learn. Being an advocate for Total Inclusivity requires skill, stamina and an advocacy stance. Trust is vitally important throughout the process, as it is what holds a learning community together. Without it, polarized and extremist views have a fertile breeding ground. Most important, you must trust yourself. Trust yourself to make mistakes, and to learn from them. Trust your ability to interact with all in your school community. Believe in your capacity to create a positive impact. If you feel that you don't have all the knowledge, understanding or skills required, recognise that you don't have them **yet** and commit to developing them.

This is what it will take. Individual advocacy by every member of the school in communal solidarity. Individual commitment by every member of the school to building inclusive and equitable systems and structures. Because the social ecosystems we inhabit, such as school communities, are designed by the humans within them. As such, they reflect the biases and values of those designers or those that lead the designers (Watson, 2007).

Advocates cannot solve the problem of inequitable school designs with the same methods that created the schooling ecosystem as we know it now. Transformation takes time, and if we don't meet people where they are at in their stage of development, we may push them too far out of their comfort zone. If this occurs, they are likely to retreat and reject any new initiatives that are too challenging for them to cognitively and emotionally deal with, resulting in resistant behaviours. Remember though that experiencing resistance does not lessen the importance of making progress. The rights and dignity of all are what are at stake if we do not challenge each other to do better.

Figure 10.1 captures the process of becoming a Totally Inclusive institution. When individuals exhibit mindsets and behaviours that provide conduits for change, advocates will be able to collaborate together in their school community. The effectiveness of policies and leadership that institutionalise structural conduits for change will foster shared commitment and sustainable practices.

As you look out across your current school landscape, imagine the other side of the hill, where a Totally Inclusive institution resides. What do you see, hear and feel? To climb the hill successfully, you will need to survey the land, gather your resources, develop your skills and overcome the challenges that you will undoubtedly cross along the way. It all starts with putting one foot in front of the other and holding the unwavering belief that creating a Totally Inclusive school is possible. As Gorman writes in her poem:

For there is always light, if only we're brave enough to see it.
If only we're brave enough to be it.

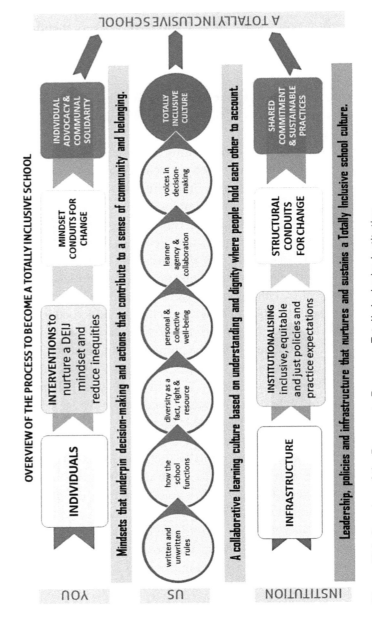

Figure 10.1 Overview of the Process to Become a Totally Inclusive Institution

As we come to the close of this book, we are thankful that you, our reader, have stayed with us through the first stage of this journey. Whilst we hope we have provided you with a useful foundation of knowledge to build on, simply reading this book is not enough. As you work to turn your knowledge into action, we strongly encourage you to use the continuum, along with the other surveys, tools and resources included. Take them as they are, or adapt them as you see fit, and begin using them to help design practical approaches and strategies that are suited to your own, unique context.

Our final advice to you as you begin the next stage of your journey to Total Inclusivity is to expect and be prepared for the ups and downs, and the highs and lows, of this important work. There will be times when the process seems to flow smoothly, when you feel heard, supported and have a reason for optimism. Enjoy and celebrate these moments and use them as fuel to keep pushing forward. Equally, be prepared for the times when the hills appear to be mountains. When you feel isolated and unsure about whether to keep going. Try not to become disheartened or discouraged by these setbacks. Keep putting one foot in front of the other. Throughout the process, take regular opportunities to reflect on the progress you have made whilst remaining mindful of the work yet to be done.

Finally, as you consider your next steps, we encourage you to ask yourself these final three reflection questions:

1. Are my actions, or those of others, promoting Total Inclusivity or perpetuating inequity?
2. Am I part of the problem or part of the solution to ending discrimination and oppression?
3. What will I do now?

(adapted from Mayfield, 2020)

Each child in our care deserves an advocate.
Will that advocate be you?

REFERENCES

Aow, A. (2021). Identity, intersectionality and inclusivity. *LinkedIn*. www.linkedin.com/pulse/identity-intersectionality-inclusivity-angeline-aow-she-her-/.

Chamorro-Premuzic, T. (2013). Why do so many incompetent men become leaders? *Harvard Business Review*. www.hbr.org/2013/08/why-do-so-many-incompetent-men.

Culture Amp. (n.d.). Homepage. Culture Amp. https://www.cultureamp.com/.

Engel, J. M. (2018). Why does culture 'eat strategy for breakfast'? *Forbes*. www.forbes.com/sites/forbescoachescouncil/2018/11/20/why-does-culture-eat-strategy-for-breakfast/?sh=40a42f3b1e09.

Fook, J. (2002). *Social Work: Critical Theory and Practice*. London: Sage.

Garmston, R. J. (2018). *The Astonishing Power of Storytelling: How Leaders and Presenters Persuade*. Thousand Oaks: Corwin.

GEC. (n.d.). The app - global equality collective. https://thegec.org/theapped.

Glanville, R. (2013). Cybernetics: Thinking Through the Technology. In D. Arnold (eds.) *Traditions of Systems Theory: Major Figures and Contemporary Developments* (pp. 45–77). New York: Routledge.

Hammer, M. R. (2012/2021). *The Intercultural Development Inventory (IDI) Resource Guide (RG)*. Hammer Holdings Incorporated.

Hattie, J. (2015). *What Doesn't Work in Education: The Politics of Distraction*. London: Pearson.

Huang, J. (2021). DEIJ missteps and how to get back on track towards liberation. *Medium*. www.huangjaz.medium.com/deij-missteps-and-how-to-get-back-on-track-towards-liberation-86122fd3982b.

Hurt, K. (2021). KPIs: The problem with key performance indicators (and what to do instead). *Let's Grow Leaders*. www.letsgrowleaders.com/2012/12/12/the-problem-with-kpis/.

Kim, M. M. J. (2021). *Wake Up: Closing the Gap between Good Intentions and Real Change*. New York: Hachette Books.

Liu, J. (2021). Read the full text of Amanda Gorman's inaugural poem 'The Hill We Climb'. *CNBC*. www.cnbc.com/2021/01/20/amanda-gormans-inaugural-poem-the-hill-we-climb-full-text.html.

Mayfield, V. (2020). *Cultural Competence Now: 56 Exercises to Help Educators Understand and Challenge Bias, Racism, and Privilege*. Alexandria, VA: ASCD.

Merriam-Webster (n.d.). Ecosystem. *Merriam-Webster*. www.merriam-webster.com/dictionary/ecosystem.

Mitchell, K. L. (n.d.). Resources. Inquiry Partners. https://www.inquirypartners.com/resources.

Neville, S. (2019). Why inclusion means getting comfortable with discomfort. *Forbes*. https://www.forbes.com/sites/ellevate/2020/12/30/why-inclusion-means-getting-comfortable-with-discomfort/?sh=1840d3a75d68.

Obama, B. (2008). Barack Obama's Feb. 5 speech. *The New York Times*. www.nytimes.com/2008/02/05/us/politics/05text-obama.html.

OECD (2012). Measuring Regulatory Performance: A Practitioner's Guide to Perception Surveys. *OECD iLibrary*. www.oecd-ilibrary.org/governance/measuring-regulatory-performance_9789264167179-en.

OECD/UIS/Eurostat (2020). Education at a Glance 2020: OECD Indicators. *OECD iLibrary*. www.oecd-ilibrary.org/sites/27f5f9c5-en/index.html?itemId=%2Fcontent%2Fcomponent%2F27f5f9c5-en.

Okun, T. (2021). White Supremacy Culture Characteristics. *White Supremacy Culture.* www.whitesupremacyculture.info/characteristics.html.

Rodberg, S. (2019, January 11). Data Was Supposed to Fix the U.S. Education System. Here's Why It Hasn't. *Harvard Business Review.* www.hbr.org/2019/01/data-was-supposed-to-fix-the-u-s-education-system-heres-why-it-hasnt.

Safir, S., & Dugan, J. (2021). *Street data: A next-generation model for equity, pedagogy, and School Transformation* (pp. 53, 62). Thousand Oaks, CA: Corwin.

Singleton, G. E. (2006/2014). *Courageous Conversations about Race: A Field Guide for Achieving Equity in Schools.* Thousand Oaks, CA: Corwin.

Slade, S. (2019). Education is an ecosystem. *ASCD.* www.ascd.org/blogs/education-is-an-ecosystem.

Stories that Move. (2016). History of the project. *Stories that Move.* www.storiesthatmove.org/en/history-of-the-project-2/.

UHLALA Group. (n.d.). Find out how LGBT+ friendly you are as an employer. https://uhlala.com/en/how-lgbt-friendly-are-you-as-an-employer/.

Watson, R. T. (2007). Information Systems. *Global Text Project.* http://ufdcimages.uflib.ufl.edu/AA/00/01/17/04/00001/InformationSystems.pdf.

YouthTruth Student Survey – A National Non-profit. (2021). Products & Services. https://youthtruthsurvey.org/products-services/.

Milton Keynes UK
Ingram Content Group UK Ltd.
UKHW052012170624
444208UK00016B/301